T0106336

# A YEAR OF FEASTING

Manual on the Seven Feasts of God Seen
From a Christian-Messianic Jewish Perspective
from the Old and New Testament

## SONYA A. MOZINGO

Copyright © 2014 Sonya A. Mozingo.

All rights reserved. No part of this book may be used or reproduced by any means, graphic, electronic, or mechanical, including photocopying, recording, taping or by any information storage retrieval system without the written permission of the publisher except in the case of brief quotations embodied in critical articles and reviews.

Archway Publishing books may be ordered through booksellers or by contacting:

Archway Publishing
1663 Liberty Drive
Bloomington, IN 47403
www.archwaypublishing.com
1-(888)-242-5904

Because of the dynamic nature of the Internet, any web addresses or links contained in this book may have changed since publication and may no longer be valid. The views expressed in this work are solely those of the author and do not necessarily reflect the views of the publisher, and the publisher hereby disclaims any responsibility for them.

Any people depicted in stock imagery provided by Thinkstock are models, and such images are being used for illustrative purposes only.
Certain stock imagery © Thinkstock.

ISBN: 978-1-4808-0653-5 (sc)
ISBN: 978-1-4808-0652-8 (e)

Library of Congress Control Number: 2014905923

Printed in the United States of America

Archway Publishing rev. date: 08/04/2014

# Dedication and Acknowledgements

I WOULD LIKE TO ACKNOWLEDGE a few important people that have strongly inspired me throughout the hardest season of my life:

I thank my Father God first and foremost. This book was written for you. It is my hope that this book will inspire your people to keep your feasts and be prosperous and blessed as a result. May all the glory, praise and honor be given to you. Rev. Larry Huch's book, Free At Last, Breaking Free from Generational Curses began a process of healing and restoration for me and my family. A family friend, Rev. Marty Mason, introduced me to Rev. Larry Huch's book, The Torah Blessing, which began my passion for reconnecting to our Jewish roots and the Feast of God, thus inspiring me to write this manual, *A Year of Feasting*. The Rev. Mike Warrick, allowed God to use him and his ministry to be instrumental in healing my brokenness. A special thank you goes to Johnathan R. Miller for helping me organize and compile this manual; you are a part of our family. I'm so grateful for my mom, Helen Autry and sister, Lori Fowler for their strong support. I also want to express gratitude to my Pastor, David Taylor and the church congregation of Oak Grove for allowing me to teach and bring the Feast of God to our community. Thank you Drue, Kayla, Jonathan and Seth, my wonderful family for hanging in there; what Satan intended for bad, God used to bring beauty out of the ashes. He doesn't waste a single life experience. I'm so grateful we didn't give up!

# Contents

## Introduction

## Part One: Highlights of the Feasts

## Part Two: The Feast Of God

## Part Three: Resources & Materials

# INTRODUCTION

# Frequently Asked Questions and Answers

Genesis 1:14 And God said, Let there be lights in the firmament of the heaven to divide the day from the night; and let them be for signs, and for seasons, and for days, and years: (KJV)

THE PUREST TRANSLATION OF THE word of God would be in the Hebrew translation, as Jesus Christ was Jewish, and most likely spoke Hebrew or Western Aramaic. Sometimes a word can have a different meaning when translated into a different language. The word for *seasons* in the Hebrew is moadim. It was not referring to the seasons such as winter, spring, summer, or fall, as most might interpret. The word moadim in Hebrew meant appointed times, the Seasons of the Lord or times for God's appearances. Now as we look at Leviticus 23:1 it reads,

> "AND THE Lord spake unto Moses, saying, Speak unto the children of Israel, and say unto them, concerning the feasts of the Lord, which ye shall proclaim to be holy convocations, even these are my feasts." (KJV)

God continues on through the entire chapter to describe the *feasts of the Lord*, which ye shall proclaim *in their seasons*. [Verse 4] KJV[1]

As we see in the scripture, God's feasts are *His* appointed times or

---

1   Refer to Verse Four

*seasons.* These are specific times that God himself put in place for his appearances. They are his very rhythm and heart beat. These feasts and seasons of God are his blueprint to keep his children prosperous, joyful and free from bondage. If we get off track, the feasts will pull us back into rhythm. This brings us to the first question:

## Do The Feasts Apply To Me Since I am Not Jewish?

Jesus Christ declares in Lev. 23: 1 that these are *his feasts*, not Jewish feasts, although the Jewish people do keep the feast as they are heirs to the covenant. The Jew's are God's chosen people and heirs to the covenant given to Abraham. But the minute we become believers in Yeshua Jesus Christ, we too are adopted into the family of Abraham, Isaac, and Jacob, and are heirs to the same covenant.

> Ephesians 2:11-14 says: "Don't forget that you are Gentiles. In fact, you used to be called "uncircumcised" by those who take pride in being circumcised. At that time you did not know about Christ. You were foreigners to the people of Israel, and you had no part in the promise that God had made to them. You were living in this world without hope and without God, and you were far from God. But Christ offered his life's blood as a sacrifice and brought you near God. Christ has made peace between Jews and Gentiles, and he has united us by breaking down the wall of hatred that separated us. (CEV)

If you have asked Jesus Christ into your heart, believe he died on the cross to save you from your sins, and confess him as Lord and savior of your life; you too are grafted into the family and heirs to the same covenant by adoption. Sure God can bless us at any time, but these are appointed times He established himself and put in place. God has a date with you. Don't stand him up!

## If I Do Not Observe the Feasts of God, Will I Still Go To Heaven?

Romans 10:9 says,

> "…That if thou shalt confess with thy mouth the Lord Jesus, and shalt believe in thine heart that God hath raised him from the dead, thou shalt be saved." (KJV)

John 14: 6 also says,

> "Jesus saith unto him, I am the way, the truth, and the life: no man comes unto the father, but by me." (KJV)

These verses clearly tell us that the only requirement to get to heaven is to confess with your mouth and believe with your heart; although Deuteronomy 6: 1-3 says,

> "These ARE the commands, decrees and laws the Lord your God directed me to teach you to observe in the land that you are crossing the Jordan to possess, so that you, your children and their children after them may fear the Lord your God as long as you live by keeping all his decrees and commands that I give you, and so that you may enjoy long life. Hear, O Israel, and be careful to obey so that it may go well with you and that you may increase, greatly in a land flowing with milk and honey, just as the Lord, the God of Your fathers, promised you." (NIV)

You see, if we love God, we will want to do what is important to him. The feasts are the very heartbeat and rhythm of God. They help the believer to stay free from bondage by keeping us in rhythm, in a pattern and on track. If we sin or get off track, as we are all human, the feast pulls us back into rhythm. Observing the feast also brings tremendous blessing. You see, you can be saved and still live with a lot of guilt and baggage from past mistakes.

God wants to continually keep us flowing in freedom and abundance. His plan from the beginning was to give us the kingdom! He can bless us at any time He chooses; but the feasts are appointed times during the year He specifically chose to bring blessing and freedom. The sun in the sky is always present, but during certain times of the year it is closer to the earth, just as God is always present—there are also specific times during the year he chooses to come close to mankind. This is by his choosing. The feasts and seasons of God is not a mere coincidence, but by sheer design.

## Am I Required to Bring an Offering to the Feast?

> "…and they shall not appear before the Lord empty: Every man shall give as he is able, according to the blessing of the Lord thy God which he hath given thee. Deuteronomy 16: 13-17 (KJV)

We all know that we are to bring our tithes and offerings to God. We are all familiar with giving our tithes, which is the first 10% of our wages. I was always taught that our offerings are what we give above and beyond our tithes. But in fact, the offerings are actually referring to the three times a year you come before the Lord and you don't come empty handed. These three offering times are during the feast of God: At the Feast of Passover, Feast of Pentecost, and the Feast of Tabernacles. These offerings should be something we anticipate and plan for ahead of time. We should cheerfully give back to God. God says with whatever measure you use to bring your offering, he will use to repay. You cannot out give God.

## Do I Have to Always Observe the Feast in This Manner?

No, this is just the way God inspired me. When God started revealing the feasts to me, my children were nearly grown and out of the house. I realized I had not taught the feast to my children, as the Bible had instructed. I had little time to make a lasting impression. The feast had to be interesting, fun and informative. I realized there were many people besides myself that did not have knowledge of the feasts of God. I wanted this manual to be of assistance to basically any size group, especially church groups, as I have used this manual in teaching in my own church. One can be as elaborate or simple as they want. As you study the feast, you will find there is endless information. You may feel you know all there is to know, only to discover God revealing something new that you had not seen before. Use the information I have compiled to make your own script or simply use the script I have provided. May God richly bless your life for being obedient to His word.

# How God Healed My Family and How I Became Familiar with the Feast

ONE MIGHT DESCRIBE MY LIFE as just average. Nothing particularly stood out. We just went to work every day and tried to raise our children the best way we knew how. People would look at me and my husband and say we had the perfect family. We are both very involved in church. My husband is a deacon, usher, recording man, church van driver, yard maintenance guy and whatever else is needed. I have worked with young people for many years and sing on the praise and worship team.

We are both very active in the community and with family and friends. The outer shell of our family appeared sound but the inside was crumbling from its foundation. Like everyone else, our family was not without its problems. Matter of fact, it was full of problems, tension, anger, rage and dislike, yes that's right…dislike. No one could stand being there. But that is not the subject of this book so I will try to give you just an overall summary of how this book came about without too much detail. In essence I had reached a crossroad in my life and was fixing to take a wrong turn.

I felt like everything was crumbling around me. Like a volcano fixing to erupt, there was a churning of emotion and a feeling of uneasiness that seemed to have become a normal emotion. I felt unhappy, unloved, unappreciated and taken for granted, resentful and angry. I was constantly simmering and ready to spew; for which I did at any given moment, on anyone who might be unlucky enough to be in my line of fire. I reached a place of desperation. I knew it would take an act of God to solve the problems we had caused in our marriage. We were beyond repair—or so I thought. I had no love left. I was done with it all. I had been crying out to God for help and direction, for years—twenty three to be exact. I was tired and fed up and tired.

One day while I was at home by myself, God got my attention in a big way. But then again—He is God! He specializes in fixing the unfixable and repairing the seemingly un-repairable. I know God must smile when we finally reach the place where we give up and turn it all over to him? He specializes in fixing what we have made a real mess of. That's when He does his best work, so that there is absolutely no question that it was the hand of God.

All of the anger and resentment I had bottled up inside had caused wounds on my soul. You see a person is made up of a body, soul, and spirit. When one gives their heart to the Lord Jesus Christ, their spirit is perfected but their soul and body is not. It is still a mess and has imperfections. Sin causes a wound on the soul. It can be sins that you committed yourself or sins caused by someone else. But these wounds can become a monument that we revisit daily. These wounds are gateways or open doors for Satan.

Even though we feel we have moved on, our minds can dwell on that hurt and begin to harbor hatred, anger and resentment. These negative emotions can cause stress that affects the body in the form of infirmities or sickness. It can also affect the soul and emotions, causing depression, etc. The more wounds you acquire, the more baggage you carry around; thus the more bondage. Wounds are like an open sore. We can try to cover them up with a band-aid, hoping it will heal over time. But if there is no real forgiveness and healing, it continues to occasionally fester.

If God doesn't heal the wound, it gives Satan legal access to the area, bringing hatred, resentment, anger, malice and the like. Satan is a liar and tries to convince us that we have moved on and are "over it"; and since there is a scab, things must be fine—right? When in fact, we are harboring these emotions and are building up inside of us hatred, pride, anger and resentment, that result in iniquities that are passed on to our children. We can be believers, forgiven of the sin but still living in bondage to the iniquities of our sin. Iniquities is tendency or a weakness in a person that attracts or pulls us toward a negative behavior.

God got my attention and showed me the problems my family was dealing with, was what the Bible calls generational curses. God gave us a pathway or guideline to follow in the Bible; these guidelines were the Ten Commandments. If we follow them, the Bible says our lives will be saturated with blessings. If we choose not to follow them, consequences for our decisions or" curses" will follow. Deuteronomy 11:26-28 Behold, I set before you this day a blessing and a curse; A blessing, if ye obey the commandments of the Lord your God, which I command you this day: And a curse, if ye will not obey the commandments of the Lord your God, but turn aside out of the way which I command you this day, to go after other gods, which ye have not known. (KJV)

We not only receive the consequences from our choices, but they can be passed on to our children and their children as well. In The Bible, Exodus 34:6-7 says the iniquities of the father can be passed onto the children to the third and fourth generation.

> "And the Lord passed by before him, and proclaimed, The Lord, The LORD God, merciful and gracious, longsuffering, and abundant in goodness and truth, Keeping mercy for thousands, forgiving iniquity and transgression and sin, and that will by no means clear the guilty; visiting the iniquity of the fathers upon the children, and upon the children's children, unto the third and to the fourth generations. Exodus 34:6-7 (KJV)

So it is not the sin of the father that passes, but the iniquity. If we ask God to forgive the sin, it is erased but the iniquity can still be passed on *if* we do not address it. God provided a way by Jesus Christ dying on a tree and shedding his blood on the cross to break the iniquity as well; so we could be totally free, not just free from sin but free from the total legality of the sin.

For instance, an alcoholic may ask God to forgive him of his sin, but even though the sin is erased, he may still struggle with the tendency to want to take another drink. And even though his children grow up saying, "I am never going to be that way" and they see the damage alcohol can cause— they end up repeating the same cycle because the iniquity can be passed on to the third and fourth generation. Don't get me wrong, everyone has a choice, but one can have more of a tendency to move toward a negative behavior due to an iniquity.

> "Be not deceived; God is not mocked: for whatsoever a man soweth, that shall he also reap." Galatians 6: 7 (KJV)

You may think your choices only affect you…but in fact it can impact your family for generations. The good news is that God did provide a way out of having to live with the iniquities. The sad thing is most people don't understand this so they go through life saved, but still bound.

God started teaching me about generational curses and blessings. Just as there are negative patterns that can follow a family's life, the same applies when we are obedient to God's word—blessing upon blessing seem to heap upon the life of the person that follows God's pathway. They are given favor and blessing. The commands God gave the people to follow in the Old Testament are considered by many to be legalistic rules followed just to receive salvation. But the word "law" in Hebrew is pathway.

The laws were not meant to be a set of legalistic rules to receive salvation. God said the commandments were to be a pathway to show you how to have a good long life.

> Deuteronomy 4:40 Thou shalt keep therefore his statutes, and his commandments, which I command thee this day, that it

may go well with thee, and with thy children after thee and that thou mayest prolong thy days upon the earth, which the Lord thy God gives thee for ever. (KJV)

So following God's commands will keep you free and prosperous.

It wasn't for their salvation; he had already brought the Israelites out of bondage and freed them. Fifty days later He brought them to Mt. Sinai to give them the Ten Commandments. Just as in the New Testament Jesus Christ died on the cross to free us from bondage and fifty days later sent the Holy Spirit at Pentecost to give us power to overcome and stay free. So we see the laws were a pathway or blueprint, if you will, to keep us free. God said he did not come to do away with the law but to show you how to live it.

God knew mankind would have a tendency to fail. God loves us so much that he was not willing to leave us there without hope. He sent his son to die on the cross to pay the price for our sin and to break the curse of the sin (or iniquities—consequences of our sin) off of our lives so that we would not have to stay in bondage from the sin. John 8:32 says that when we recognize and understand the truth, the truth that we understand is what sets us free.

Because of this truth, when you accept Jesus Christ into your heart—he not only forgives you of the sin, but now the negative patterns (iniquities) can also be broken off of your life and can be halted and not passed on to your children and their children to the third and fourth generation. God said My people are destroyed for lack of knowledge. [Hosea 4:6] (KJV)[2]

Most believers don't understand what Jesus Christ did on the cross and therefore continue to live their life saved from their sin but still in bondage to that sin. There are consequences for your choices. If this is never acknowledged and dealt with and brought before God to

---

2   Hosea 4:6-My people are destroyed for lack of knowledge: because thou hast rejected knowledge, I will also reject thee, that thou shalt be no priest to me: seeing thou hast forgotten the law of thy God, I will also forget thy children. King James Version (KJV)

forgive and reverse, you will continue to carry it throughout your life. When a person thinks about their salvation, they think of a date that they gave their heart to the Lord Jesus Christ. But the Bible says in 1 Corinthians 1:18

> "For the message of the cross is foolishness to those who are perishing, but to us who are *being* saved it is the power of God." (NIV)

We are being saved (or in this context so-zoed [Greek]), which means we are constantly being healed, being forgiven, being saved, this is an ongoing process. Most people stop after asking God to forgive them of their sin but he wants you free *indeed* free and on top of that, free from the bondage of that sin.

But it doesn't stop there, once free from bondage—how do we stay free? This brings us to where we are now. God started revealing the Feast of the Lord and holy days to me in a new light, I was getting the big picture. This was also part of God's blueprint to stay free and prosperous. When we accept Jesus Christ into our hearts we are grafted into the family of Abraham, Isaac, and Jacob and are therefore entitled to the same covenant blessing still in effect today. God made it available to us as well. By keeping his commandments, feasts, and holy days, God's blessing, abundance and favor is promised even to us.

You see it was God's plan from the very beginning of time, when he created Adam and Eve. He wanted His people to be happy, prosperous and free. One doesn't have to remember the feasts and holy days to go to heaven; you simply receive Jesus Christ as your Lord and savior. If you want to be an air to the covenant blessing and receive the entirety of God's promise, then we have to follow His blueprint or pathway for our life.

Accept Jesus Christ into your heart and believe that he died on the cross for your sins. Then confess He is Lord of your life. This confession of your belief will get you into heaven. Secondly, He wants you free. God starting showing me there were a lot of believers that are walking around free from sin, but are still in bondage; they are going to heaven but living and dealing with situations from bad decisions or choices in their past. He wants His people free. The one word God kept revealing to me during my own crisis was freedom. The way to do that is to recognize the negative pattern or iniquity on our life. Repent for the sin.

Separate the sin from the person, and forgive the person. (This frees you) Forgive yourself for any part. Ask God to cover you and the iniquity with the blood of Calvary (because he died on the cross-his death on the cross and shed blood breaks the curse). Recognize and ask God to break the curse of—(whatever it is), and repent for the sin (even repent for the sin of past generations that is connected to you)-ask God to let the blood of Calvary cover you and the negative pattern on your life.-then replace it with blessing. (Or the opposite of the negative pattern) Ask God to reverse the sin and to seal that wound forever with the blood of Calvary.

Then finally stay free and prosperous by remembering the Sabbath and keeping His feasts and holy days. This is a sure formula established by God himself. It was given so that his people could live a life of fullness and prosperity and not only be free but free indeed!

The rest of the pages of this book are devoted to helping you have an understanding of the feast and how you can remember and commemorate them. You and your family can simply follow the feast as they are written in the book by using this manual or simply glean from the information and come up with your own script or way of commemorating.

It was designed to be used by churches or groups or families. You can decorate as elaborate as you wish or not at all. My intent was to make the feast interesting, beautiful, remember able and informative while keeping a simple menu. I wanted to add a feel of Jewish culture to bridge the gap and add an element of fun. I hope you look forward to keeping the feast as I have, as we delight in doing what God has instructed and, while watching his promises come to pass in our own lives.

I believe as we do the will of God, we are bridging the gap between God's children, the Jew and Gentile that

"...they all (Jew and Gentile) may be one...that the world may believe..." John 17:21 (NIV)

Christ has made peace between Jews and Gentiles, and he has united us by breaking down the wall of hatred that separated us...And because of Christ, all of us can come to the Father by the same Spirit. Ephesians 2: 14-18 (CEV)[3]

---

3   Christ has made peace between Jews and Gentiles, and he has united us by breaking down the wall of hatred that separated us. Christ gave his own body 15 to destroy the Law of Moses with all its rules and commands. He even brought Jews and Gentiles together as though we were only one person, when he united us in peace. 16 On the cross Christ did away with our hatred for each other. He also made peace[a] between us and God by uniting Jews and Gentiles in one body. 17 Christ came and preached peace to you Gentiles, who were far from God, and peace to us Jews, who were near God. 18 And because of Christ, all of us can come to the Father by the same Spirit. Ephesians 2: 14-18 (CEV)

# PART ONE:
# HIGHLIGHTS OF THE FEASTS

# Highlights of Passover, Unleavened Bread, and Firstfruits

And this day shall be unto you for a memorial; and ye shall keep it a feast to the Lord throughout your generations; ye shall keep it a feast by an ordinance forever. Exodus 12:14 (KJV)

In the fourteenth day of the first month at even is the Lord's Passover. And on the fifteenth day of the same month is the feast of unleavened bread unto the Lord; seven days ye must eat unleavened bread … When ye be come into the land which I give unto you, and shall reap the harvest, thereof, then ye shall bring a sheaf of the firstfruits of your harvest unto the priest. Leviticus 23:5–10 (KJV)

## What Is the Feast of Passover All About?

THE PASSOVER FEAST IS THE first feast celebrated in the spring, along with the Feast of Unleavened Bread and the Feast of Firstfruits. The Passover Feast is a time of remembering how God delivered the Israelites out of bondage from Egypt by putting the blood of a spotless lamb over the door of their homes. This is a beautiful picture of Jesus Christ giving his own life and becoming the ultimate spotless lamb and taking away the sin of the world and making a way to free mankind from the bondage of sin. The feast is usually commemorated by doing a Seder meal (an object lesson using various foods and Bible Scripture to describe how God delivered and freed the Israelites), which is observed usually on the first and second days of a seven-day period. During the entire seven days, only matzo (bread without leaven) is eaten. *No bread that has risen will be eaten for the entire week* in remembrance of the Feast of Unleavened Bread.

Women begin cooking and using up the things made with leaven in the weeks before Passover. They start cleaning up their houses, sweeping the floors, and cleaning under the cushions to rid the house of any morsels of leaven. Some give the items of food that contain leaven, and are not eaten prior to the feast, to the needy, but they get it out of their house for the duration of the seven days. Leaven is symbolic of sin in our lives. Pride and sin make us puffed up like leaven makes bread puff up.

The Feast of Unleavened Bread causes us to check our lives, repent, and rid ourselves of our arrogant and prideful ways. The Feast of Firstfruits usually takes place the day after the Passover Feast. It was when a sheaf of barley was brought and waved before the Lord. The Lord's acceptance was a pledge on his part to bring a full harvest. For believers, it reminds us that everything we have comes from God, and if we are obedient to bring our firstfruit offering (which is the first of three offerings during the year), then he is faithful to take our offering, bless it, and return it to us with abundance.

Therefore, we see a combination of three different feasts in that one-week observance: the Feast of Passover, the Feast of Unleavened Bread, and the Feast of Firstfruit.

## What Is Required?

Exodus 12—Bitter herbs (horseradish is used a lot), unleavened bread (bread made without yeast), and a spotless lamb (an unbroken bone of a lamb is kept and used from year to year by many to remember the spotless lamb).

No customary work on it

Deuteronomy 6—we are to teach ourselves, our children, and our grandchildren to keep his feast and holy days, and to pass them on from generation to generation. Teach these statutes that we may enjoy long life and increase greatly just as the Lord, the God of your fathers, promised you.

Deuteronomy 6:20–25 says:

> "In the future. when your son asks you, "What is the meaning of the stipulations, decrees and laws the Lord our God has commanded you?" tell him: "We were slaves of Pharaoh in Egypt, but the Lord brought us out of Egypt with a mighty hand, Before our eyes the Lord sent miraculous signs and wonders great and terrible-upon Egypt and Pharaoh and his whole household. But he brought us out from there to bring us in and give us the land that he promised on oath to our forefathers. The Lord commanded us to obey all these decrees and to fear the Lord our God so that we might always prosper and be kept alive, as is the case today. And if we are careful to obey all this law before the Lord our God, as he has commanded us, that will be our righteousness." (NIV)

Passover means "protection." Passover refers to instructions given by God to those marked with blood. If we obey God and align ourselves up with his plan, he promises in Exodus 23 that he will do the following:

1. Assign you an angel,
2. Be an enemy to your enemies,
3. Give you prosperity,
4. Take away sickness,
5. Give you long life,
6. Bring increase and inheritance to you, and
7. Give you a special year of blessing.

## Things to Remember

Teach your children how God delivered his people by using bitter herbs, unleavened bread, and a spotless lamb. Do no work on the first and the seventh days, and give your first firstfruit offering.

Things typically seen on a Jewish family's table: the Seder meal, no bread with leaven.

# Highlights of Pentecost

"From the day after the Sabbath, the day you brought the sheaf of the wave offering, count off seven full weeks. Count off fifty days up to the day after the seventh Sabbath, and then present an offering of new grain to the Lord. Leviticus 23:15–16 (NIV)

## What Is Shavuot/the Feast of Pentecost All About?

SHAVUOT CELEBRATES THE INGATHERING OF the first harvest. At the Feast of Ingathering, people brought baskets filled with fig, grapes, pomegranate, wheat, barley, olives, and dates. They knew it was seedtime (time to bring the very best firstfruits of their crop) as an offering to God so that he would open the windows of heaven and pour them out a blessing.

The first thing in season was barley. The people would wave two loaves of barley before the Lord. The priest would lift them up to God, symbolizing the coming abundance and the miracle harvest promised during this season. During the Feast of Weeks, or Pentecost, we too are to bring our second of three "firstfruit" offerings to the Lord. Also on the Day of Pentecost, as seen in the New Testament, the Holy Spirit was poured out on the first church in the upper room in Jerusalem; three thousand people were born again.

This was the "first harvest" unto the Lord. In contrast, in the Old Testament, the first Shavuot, or Day of Pentecost, was when the Holy Spirit was poured out at Mount Sinai and the Ten Commandments were given; this occurred fifty days after the Israelites had been delivered out of bondage in Egypt.

In the New Testament, the Messiah came and died on the cross and rose from the dead to remove the bondage and slavery from our lives. Exactly fifty days later, when the day of Pentecost was fully come, they were all in one accord in one place and the Holy Spirit, as fire, sat upon each of them [Acts 2:13–21][4]. Hence, the number fifty is very important. It means "jubilee."

The people received a double-portion blessing and God canceled their debt. Upon receiving the Holy Spirit, he makes us righteous in him by writing the laws on our heart. Pentecost was more than just being set free. It was God's strategy for staying free. It meant the end of bondage and a new beginning. It symbolized a covenant with God or a marriage to him. Shavuot, or Pentecost, brings the entire spring feast to a full end. It is the final feast connected with Yeshua's First Coming. The remaining feast in the fall is linked to the Second Coming of the Lord.

---

4   14 Then Peter stood up with the Eleven, raised his voice and addressed the crowd: "Fellow Jews and all of you who live in Jerusalem, let me explain this to you; listen carefully to what I say. 15 These people are not drunk, as you suppose. It's only nine in the morning! 16 No, this is what was spoken by the prophet Joel:

17 "'In the last days, God says,
   I will pour out my Spirit on all people.
Your sons and daughters will prophesy,
   your young men will see visions,
   your old men will dream dreams.
18 Even on my servants, both men and women,
   I will pour out my Spirit in those days,
   and they will prophesy.
19 I will show wonders in the heavens above
   and signs on the earth below,
   blood and fire and billows of smoke.
20 The sun will be turned to darkness
   and the moon to blood
   before the coming of the great and glorious day of the Lord.
21 And everyone who calls
   on the name of the Lord will be saved.

## What Is Required?

Have a feast unto God, in which we bring an offering to the Lord (the second of three for the year) and proclaim that it is a holy convocation and do no customary work.

## Things to Remember

Pentecost was the end of bondage and the beginning of freedom. Pentecost was God's strategy for staying free by giving us the gift of the Holy Spirit. The Holy Spirit has many great qualities, such as these: it enables us to have the boldness to tell the world about Jesus Christ and it gives us power to overcome our sins so we can be totally free.

## Things Typically Seen on a Jewish Family's Table

We can eat *about anything* we like. But dairy is always found, since this reminded them that once they received the Torah (first five books of the Old Testament), they were like babies who drank only milk. They usually eat blintzes or cheese kreplach (dumplings), Jewish crepes, or *cheesecake*. (Of course, pork and shellfish would not be served.)

The Ten Commandments are usually read at the feast. The book of Ruth can be read at feast time, as it teaches loyalty, tolerance, and love for one another.

## Recommendations and Ideas for Feast—but Not Required

Include loaves of wheat bread, which was the new grain. Have trays containing the seven fruits mentioned in Deuteronomy 8:8, which spoke of a land of wheat, barley, vines (grapes and fig), pomegranates, olive oil (olives), dates, and honey to remind them of a bountiful harvest. Include lots of dairy items.

# Highlights of Rosh Hashanah/ Feast of Trumpets

Speak unto the children of Israel, saying, In the seventh month, in the first day of the month, shall ye have a sabbath rest, a memorial of blowing of trumpets, an holy convocation. Leviticus 23:24 (KJV)

## What Is Rosh Hashanah, or the Feast of Trumpets All About?

ROSH HASHANAH WELCOMES IN GOD'S New Year with the blowing of a shofar and a time of soul searching and reflection. Thirty days leading up to the time of Rosh Hashanah, known as the month of Tishre, begins with searching our heart. Ask God to reveal areas in which we need forgiveness and to show us areas of bitterness, anger, resentment and pride that need to be addressed. Ask God to reveal to us people that we need to seek forgiveness from. Ask God to reveal sin in our lives or areas of hurt that need mending.

Following the month of Tishre is Rosh Hashanah, a ten day period in which we make amends with people we have wronged or have wronged us. Ask ourselves, "Have we been tithing? Have we treated others with respect? Have we treated others the way we want to be treated? Am I following the Ten Commandments? Do I harbor hurt, bitterness, anger or hatred? It is a time for true repentance. It is believed that God's book of blessing is opened and "He "is examining our heart and our TRUE intentions. We may act a certain way to others, but God knows our true intentions and motives. He is giving us an opportunity to come clean before a Holy and all knowing God. The time leading up to Rosh Hashanah is a time to refresh and renew our lives; start a new beginning. If we come clean before God he will write our name in the Book of Blessing and seal us for a good year, as this is the beginning of the New Year on God's calendar.

But If He decides to tarry, and delay His coming; it is thought that His return could be during the Feast of Trumpets. It is also during this feast that we celebrate the anniversary of creation, or should we say the birthday of Adam and Eve. This feast is about God doing a new thing.

He wants to wipe the slate clean and give us a fresh start. The sounding of the shofar is calling us to be ready for the rapture of the church and; if He chooses to delay his coming, He wants to erase the sin from our lives and give us a good, prosperous and full year.

## What is Required?

- » The blowing of the shofar
- » Ten days of soul searching
- » In the seventh month, on the first day of the month a Sabbath rest, a holy convocation-no customary work

## Things to Remember

Search your heart and find forgiveness. Rid your lives of sin, anger, greed, unforgiveness, pride and arrogance. Blow the shofar and get ready for the coming of Jesus Christ.

## Things typically seen on a Jewish family's table

*Apple dipped in honey*—to symbolize our desire for a sweet year

*Classic honey cake*—to represent the sweetness of God and how good and merciful he is to forgive us of sin (recipes can be found on line)

*Challah bread baked in a circle*—as a wish or hope that the coming year will roll around smoothly without unhappiness or sorrow and that our year will be blessed

*Pomegranate*—is eaten symbolizing our wish to have a year *full* of good deeds, as a pomegranate is filled with many, many luscious seeds.

*Sweet potato dishes*—symbolizes our desire for a sweet year

*Carrot dishes*—in Yiddish the word for carrot means to multiply. It is our hope that God will bless us richly and will greatly multiply an abundance of blessings, and open the windows of heaven over us.

*Head of a fish*—symbolizes our desire to be the head and not the tail, the lender and not the borrower, above and not beneath and in a leading position-we are blessed of God!

*They find a pool or body of water in which they throw crumbs into the water. This symbolizes that they are casting away sins or the "old man." This reminded God's people while visiting a body of water like a river or pond with fish in it; that fish are dependent on water and we are dependent on God. A fish's eye's never close. God doesn't sleep and is always watching over us. We are leaving our old ways behind us, and starting a new year with a clean slate. God will cast our sin into the sea of forgetfulness, never to be remembered again!

# Highlights of the Day of Atonement

And the Lord spake unto Moses, saying, Also on the tenth day of this seventh month there shall be a day of atonement: it shall be a holy convocation unto you; and ye shall afflict your souls, and offer an offering made by fire unto the Lord. And ye shall do no work in that same day; for it is a day of atonement, to make an atonement for you before the Lord your God. Leviticus 23: 26-28 (KJV)

## What is the Day of Atonement All About?

THE DAY OF ATONEMENT IS the most holy day on God's calendar. The word atonement broken up is "at one." God wants intimacy with his people. In the Old Testament, the Day of Atonement was a time when the priest would offer a sacrifice for the sins of the people. Now that Jesus Christ has died on the cross for our sin, He has become the ultimate sacrifice and we no longer sacrifice animals. But we offer ourselves as a living sacrifice, holy and acceptable before God. It is so very, very, very important to remember what Jesus Christ did for us on this day; and to fast for the day, out of honor and respect for Him—as this is considered the most holy day on God's calendar.

## What is Required?

Afflict our souls, or fast on the Day of Atonement and do not work

## Things to Remember

Yom Kippur or the Day of Atonement is the holiest day on God's calendar. Fast, pray and repent. Find forgiveness and give forgiveness.

# Highlights of the Feast of Tabernacles/Sukkot

Thou shalt observe the feast of tabernacles seven days, after that thou hast gathered in thy corn and thy wine. And thou shalt rejoice in thy feast, thou, and thy son, and thy daughter….Seven days shalt thou keep a solemn feast unto the Lord thy God in the place which the Lord shall choose: because the Lord thy God shall bless thee in all thine increase, and in all the works of thine hands, therefore thou shalt surely rejoice….and they shall not appear before the Lord empty: Every man shall give as he is able, according to the blessing of the Lord thy God which he hath given thee. Deuteronomy 16:13-17 (KJV)

## What is Sukkot or Feast of Tabernacles All About:

THE FEAST IS A TIME that we are required to bring our final "first fruit" offering before the Lord. It is a time of harvest and abundance as this is the time for the final ingathering of crops. This feast reminds us of Thanksgiving, being thankful for their crops and for His atonement and a new beginning. Lights are one of the things that distinguish this feast from others, as we know Jesus Christ is the light of the world. It is a time to remember the Israelites living in booths or small tabernacles to serve as a reminder of their temporary living conditions and how God supplied every need and healed and delivered them. He too is our healer and provider. Jesus birthday is thought to be on or near the Feast of Tabernacles, thus being a time of great joy. In this feast we see the Marriage of the Lamb, and the making of the New Covenant, and God establishing His Kingdom on earth. We see the great harvest of souls, which is a picture of the Millennium, when Christ reigns on the earth for 1000 years.

## What is Required?

> » A joyful celebration for seven days, in which the first day shall be a holy convocation and do not work. Deuteronomy 16:13-14 (KJV) and Leviticus23:40 (KJV)

> » The third and final "first fruit" offering

> » To wave the four species—a palm tree branch, myrtle branches, the willow of a tree and an etrog, before the Lord in worship Leviticus 23:40 (KJV)

> » To construct a booth or tabernacle to live in for seven days Leviticus 23:42 (KJV)

## Things to Remember

The feast is a joyful time of celebration for seven days. It is the birthday of Jesus, the light of the world. It is a time to remember God's provision by constructing a booth and rejoicing before the Lord by waiving the four species (a combination of four different plants) in six directions: north, south, east, and west, up and down, symbolizing that God is everywhere. The different plants symbolize the different parts of the body of Christ or the different kinds of Jews (in which believing Gentiles are "different" because we are grafted in) And Sukkot is a time of bringing our final "first fruit" offering before the Lord.

## Things Typically Seen On a Jewish Family's Table

Families can eat about anything, except pork or shell fish, but *stuffed foods* are extremely common. Stuffed foods are likened to miniature cornucopias, representing a bountiful harvest.

# Highlights from the Eighth Day Celebration

…on the eighth day shall be a holy convocation unto you;…
Leviticus 23:36 (KJV)

## What is the Eighth Day All About?

IT IS A SACRED AND intimate time spent with God. It is a picture of God inviting us to, "Spend one more day together." It is a time to intimately reconnect with God our creator. It is a time when the feasts have come to an end and we will be returning back to our normal lives. It is thought that Jesus Christ would have been circumcised on this day, as Jewish males were circumcised on the eighth day after birth. Circumcision represents covenant. Jesus Christ was sealing His covenant with mankind. It is a good time to review all of the feast and the blessings that go along with each feast. It is a time to honor God as He has made these specific appointed times to meet with us. We usually pursue God, but these are times that God actually makes an appointment with mankind. Don't stand God up—by missing out on all He has for you!

## What is Required?

A sacred assembly and do no work

## Suggestions But Not Required:

Have everyone make or bring a dish that pertains to one of the feasts and be prepared to describe which feast it came from and how it pertains to the feast. Example: a dish that is made of dairy—for Feast of Pentecost to show that this was a time when they were babes in Christ, a carrot dish—for Feast of Trumpets, in hopes that God would multiply their blessings, or a dish that is stuffed—for Feast of Tabernacles to represent abundance, like a jelly filled doughnut.

# PART TWO:
# THE FEAST OF GOD

# Passover, Feast of Unleavened Bread, and Firstfruits Preparation List

## Preparation and Food List:

1. Put **two tables together** so that 12 people are seated per table. Use **white paper disposable tablecloths** with beautiful centerpieces and candles. (Decorate as elaborate as you wish) Have **place settings arranged with plate, beverage glass, wine glass, silverware and napkin.** (I used clear plastic plates with plastic clear wine glasses and paper doilies under glasses).**Four small communion cups per plate can be used instead of a plastic wine glass or any plastic cup**. (If one cup is used, instruct the guest to take one sip as you will be partaking at four different times)

2. **A small card table or round table** is set up at the front and decorated to be used by the host.

3. **Two candles in holders for lighting (with matches)** are set on the front table (where the host stands) along with the **seder plate complete with elements** (This can be found on line) and four cups of wine/juice

4. **Individual small bowls or cups containing water with a napkin** -per place setting-for hand washing

5.  **Two plates per table containing matzah bread**. (Three pieces of matzah with a cloth between them-a cloth on the top, between, and one on the bottom. -Also two plates with extra pieces of matzah. (For the purpose of eating with soup)

6.  **Sprigs of parsley**, maror or bitter herbs(**horseradish**) and a mixture consisting of apples, nuts, and honey (representing brick mortar)are placed on the plate of each place setting prior to the service. Three bowls of salted water are placed on each table to dip the parsley. (People are instructed not to double dip)

7.  **Wine or grape juice** can be used for the cups. (I like to have this poured and sitting on the table prior to the arrival of guest) You can use four communion cups per guest or take four separate sips from the same cup. Just instruct the guest that they will be taking four separate sips.

8.  **Jewish music is playing** in the background to set the mood for a festive time of fellowship and to create a fun atmosphere. Our guest are seated and served a beverage (in our case we served tea, water, or coffee)

9.  **Matzah ball soup is served** (I like to serve soup as it is simple and easy and found on many Jewish tables. Recipes can be found on line. Harris Teeter usually carries packets of the soup) at the appropriate time by the servers along with two treys, per table of assorted fruit. This is prepared prior to the service and put on the tables at the instructed time so as not to distract from the message and to keep the soup hot. Tea and water refills are also given. The idea is to keep it simple. We want this to be a time to experience our Jewish heritage in a fun and exciting way, but not to overwhelm them or the ones preparing this event. Again, during the time of eating the soup and fruit, I like to play festive Jewish music to create a fun atmosphere. This is a time to fellowship together. The menu can change according to how simple you want it to be. One can get ideas from the internet.

10. **Four to six plastic water basins** per table are used for foot washing; (sharing is appropriate as one will not be submerging their foot completely) and four to six plastic pictures filled with water per table. These are brought to the tables at the appropriate time as to not be a distraction. I recommend that the women wear slacks to this event for this reason. A disposable cloth is given to each person to dry the feet. (Bottles of antiseptic cleanser are placed on the tables to be used by those that wish to do so.

11. The speaker gives the example first by pouring water over the foot of their brother into the basin beneath (They do not have to submerge the foot in the basin of water) Remember this is the example Jesus demonstrated at the last supper before he was crucified; and we should be willing and humble servants as well. Again I play soft Jewish music and maintain an atmosphere of reverence. (Families can participate together in foot washing or 2 males or 2 females)

12. After foot washing, I recommend a time of prayer and reflection. I suggest the guest find a quiet place by themselves or simply bow their heads where they are sitting to pray and seek God.

13. The **blessings**[5] **and list of plagues** are placed at each place setting for every guest.

14. Have some **small prizes** available for the kids, as they will be finding hidden matzah later in the service. The leader will ransom the matzah back in exchange for a prize.

15. Assign readers for the verses prior to starting the service.

16. A leader to represent each table (preferably a man) should be picked prior to starting the service.

17. A woman of honor is picked prior to starting the service to light the candles.

---

5   see re-printable sheets

# Feast of Passover, Unleavened Bread and First Fruits: A Season of Liberation

## (Script for Leader)

THE WORD OF GOD SPEAKS of a man whose name was Abraham. Abraham was given a promise from God. He was promised the land of Israel. He was also promised descendants as numerous as the stars in the heavens. Gentile nations would come to salvation in the same way, by the grace of God through the sinless Sacrifice Lamb he had promised. Jews and gentiles will eventually come together as one. They will be one united family. Isaiah spoke of Israel being a light to the Gentiles.[6]

Approximately 1500 B.C. was when God's servant Moses was instructed or told to lead His people out of bondage from Egypt, and not long after, God gave instruction and put in place the Seven Feast of Israel. The Bible says that these are God's feasts and are holy convocations or rehearsals of what is to come. They were to be a blue print for our lives. The feasts are the very rhythm a heartbeat of God and keep our lives on track. The feasts are to be remembered and celebrated every year—indefinitely. Three of these feast or holy days are in the spring, one in the summer, and three in the fall. It is indeed an entire full year of feasting.

---

6   Isaiah 42:6, 49:6, 60:3

These are appointed days in which God calls his people to come together from their normal everyday lives and to set aside these times for remembrance. These feasts teach God's people to learn key spiritual lessons and remember important events in history. Just as there are dress rehearsals in a play, the feasts are to be a rehearsal of what is to come. God has set up His feasts to match the dates on the Hebrew calendar and coincides to the covenant given to Abraham that exists between the God of Israel and His people. God instructs us to teach these feast to our children from generation to generation so that we will stay prepared and ready for what is to come. These feasts are God's eternal plan. God is drawing out for himself a chosen people, a remnant who are the royal priesthood. Exodus19:6 says it like this:

"And ye shall be unto me a kingdom of priests, and a holy nation. These are the words which thou shalt speak unto the children of Israel." (KJV)

1 Peter 2:9 says:

> "But ye are a chosen generation,, a royal priesthood, an holy nation, a peculiar people; that ye should show forth the praises of him who hath called you out of darkness into his marvellous light." (KJV)

God is continually redeeming his people.

In scripture we find the seven feasts of God. Seven is the number of perfection or completion. These feasts are an ancient portal to some of the richest blessings of God. So let's briefly explain the seven feasts.

The Feast of Passover in the Old Testament, commemorated the day the spotless lamb was slain and its blood was put on the door post of every Jewish home signifying a covering, thus preventing the death angel from killing the first born in their family. In the New Testament, Jesus was commemorating Passover when he was partaking in what we call the Lord's Supper right before he shed his precious blood for the sins of the world, thus becoming the ultimate Passover lamb. Passover occurs on the first and second days of the week of the Feast of Unleavened Bread. The Feast of Unleavened Bread is a time to remember Israel passing through the Red

Sea. It is also a time of removing sin and pride, which is a type of leaven, from our homes and our lives. At the end of the seven day celebration, is the Feast of First Fruits. This is when a sheaf of barley was brought into the temple and presented to the Lord. This was an offering brought to God. They brought their very best and first harvest of their crop.

1 Corinthians 15:20 says:

> But now is Christ risen from the dead, and become the firstfruits of them that slept. (KJV)

The Feast of Firstfruits was pointing to Jesus Christ resurrection. Then exactly fifty days from that time brings us to the Feast of Pentecost.

The feast of Pentecost in the Old Testament is when Moses received the Ten Commandments on Mount Sinai, fifty days after Israel passed through the Red Sea. Amazingly, in the New Testament, exactly fifty days after Jesus Christ was raised from the dead, the Holy Spirit was given—This was at Pentecost as well. Both events in the scripture had the elements of lightening, thunder and streaks of fire. God is always amazingly exact and precise.

The last three feasts are in the fall, The Feast of Rosh Hashanah, Yom Kippur, and Sukkot. These feasts are known as the high holy days. Rosh Hashanah, also known as the Feast of Trumpets, means the beginning year. Rosh Hashanah is the New Year on God's calendar. It is a time for blowing the shofar and getting ready for the coming of the Lord. The Feast of Yom Kippur otherwise known as the Day of Atonement is when a sacrifice for sin was given. Jesus Christ became the ultimate sacrifice by giving his life for mankind; and it points to the seven years of tribulation; those left behind must accept Jesus Christ as Messiah before his second coming. Sukkot, also known as the Feast of Tabernacles, points to the millennial reign of Christ on the earth when God lives with, and tabernacles with his people.

All of these feasts are found in the first five books in the scripture. These feast are for everyone who has been "grafted in" (Romans 11:17) and are an ancient portal or pathway to God's rich and abundant blessing. Each feast has its own unique blessing when we choose to honor God as he commanded. So, now that we have an understanding of what the feasts are, let's look specifically tonight at the Feast of Passover.

In Hosea 4:6 it says:

> My people (*those whose are serving him*) are destroyed (*because of one thing*) for lack of knowledge. (KJV)

To get knowledge and an accurate understanding of God's truth from scripture, we need to read the Bible from the perspective in which it was written, the Jewish world of first-century Jerusalem and surrounding Israel. Those who wrote the Bible probably spoke Hebrew, Greek, Latin, and Aramaic. But they thought and reasoned like Jewish people. So we want to take some time right now to see Jesus through Jewish eyes, because he was in fact Jewish.

*Pray*

How many of us would admit that we have family that we just don't get along with or don't quite see eye to eye. We call them family but we don't always see things the same way. Or maybe just don't understand them. Well I want us to look deep in our hearts and think about our family tree. Where DID we come from and who are we? When we think of the Jewish people, a lot of times we think of a hated people. A group of people that are very different from ourselves or perhaps someone we know very little about. We know the Jews are God's "chosen people" and heirs to the covenant given to Abraham. But, we need to understand the minute we become believers in Yeshua Jesus Christ; we too are adopted into the family of Abraham, Isaac, and Jacob, and are heirs to the same covenant. We are now a part of the family of God and are connected with Jewish descent. We now belong and are grafted into to a very wealthy family. But it is up to us- what we do with it. We just read what the word says about God's people—they perish for lack of knowledge. Our heavenly father loves us so much that he made sure we were well taken care of by providing for our every need. So much so that he even gave us a blueprint or pathway to follow to stay free and blessed. We are told to follow his commandments so that we will have a good long life. When we follow God's commandments, blessings will follow. Of course when we don't follow God's commandments, there are consequences for our actions. .He gave us instructions for the feast of God as well. Remembering God's feast brings abundant blessing

Now, how exactly do the Gentile believing world and the Jewish world fit together? To come to a better understanding of who we are and who our Jewish brother and sisters are, let's read Ephesians 2:11 from the contemporary English version

Reader # 1 Do not forget that you are Gentiles. In fact, you used to be called "uncircumcised" by those who take pride in being circumcised. At that time you did not know about Christ. You were foreigners to the people of Israel, and you had no part in the promise that God had made to them. You were living in this world without hope and without God, and you were far from God. But Christ offered his life's blood as a sacrifice and brought you near God. Christ has made peace between Jews and Gentiles, and he has united us by breaking down the wall of hatred that separated us. Christ gave his own body to destroy the Law of Moses with all its rules and commands. (the law of commandments contained in ordinances. New King James Version) He even brought Jews and Gentiles together as though we were only one person, when he united us in peace. On the cross Christ did away with our hatred for each other. He also made peace between us and God by uniting Jews and Gentiles in one body. Christ came and preached peace to you Gentiles, who were far from God, and peace to Jews, who were near God. And because of Christ, all of us can come to the Father by the same Spirit. You Gentiles are no longer strangers and foreigners. You are citizens with everyone else who belongs to the family of God. You are like a building with the apostles and prophets as the foundation and with Christ as the most important stone. Christ is the one who holds the building together and makes it grow into a holy temple for the Lord. And you are part of that building Christ has built as a place for God's own Spirit to live.

This is a lot to digest, but God wants to tear down the wall of division that separates Israel and the Gentile church. An example would be like our families that have division. Ephesians 4:13 says:

"Till we all come to the unity of the faith, and of the knowledge of the Son of God, unto a perfect man, unto the measure of the stature of the fullness of Christ." (KJV)

In other words: when we (Gentile believers) add to our faith—knowledge (an understanding of the Jewish Torah or Old Testament) and the Jews add to their knowledge—faith (a belief in Jesus as the Messiah), then we will become that one new man—perfect and complete. Christian believers understand very little about the first five books of the Bible /Torah, yet recognize Jesus Christ as the Messiah. In contrast, the Jews are the keeper of the Torah, but do not recognize that Jesus Christ is the Messiah. When both come to this understanding, we will see the fullness of Christ come about in our lives, and the temple of God will be complete.

We who are believers, who have accepted Christ as our Lord and savior, are now a part of the family. We are legal heirs to the covenant. We have been grafted into the root.

READER #2 Romans 11:17-18 says it this way in the Contemporary English version: You Gentiles are like branches of a wild olive tree that were made to be part of a cultivated olive tree. You have taken the place of some branches that were cut away from it. And because of this, you enjoy the blessings that come from being part of that cultivated tree. But don't think you are better than the branches that were cut away. Just remember that you are not supporting the roots of that tree. Its roots are supporting you.

Remember not to speak against Israel—we are the ones grafted (or adopted) into the family! A lot of times we think we have it all right and everyone else is wrong, but nobody has it all right. We both have things we need to work on. And since we are legal heirs to the Covenant—we can take part in all the blessings and fullness God has for us. He wants to give his people blessings that are shaken down and running over; so full that we can't contain it all. God wants us to have so much blessing that we have to give it away and share it with the world! We are blessed to be a blessing and we are to be a light in the darkness!

Now that we have established who we are, let's talk about the feast that we are remembering. Tonight we are actually looking at three separate feasts that are all occurring within a seven day period.

Passover occurs on the first and often second night of the seven-day period. Tonight we will be celebrating by taking part in a combined Seder meal connecting the Old and New Testaments. The Feast of First Fruit is on the next night following, and the Feast of Unleavened Bread lasts for the entire seven days. We will elaborate on each one.

We will start with the Feast of Unleavened Bread, which last for the entire week/seven days. What is leaven anyway? "Leaven" is the ingredient in bread, pastries and certain foods that make it rise or puff up. So what does leaven have to do with anything? For Jewish people, it reminds them that their deliverance from Egypt happened so quickly that there was no time to bake bread for their journey. The bread did not have time to rise. They had to just take their kneading bowls with them.

It reminded them that God provided manna for them in the desert, when they had no food. So during the seven day period, Matzah and bread that has no yeast or leaven, is the only bread eaten for the entire week. Weeks prior to the Feast of Unleavened Bread, women begin using up the things made with leaven in the house. They meticulously clean their homes clean under pillow cushions and sweep the floors, cleaning out any morsel of leaven that might be hiding. This helps them to remember to rid their hearts of sin and pride or anything that would cause them to be arrogant or puffed up. Some Jewish people give the things made with leaven to needy people, but they get it out of their houses for the duration of seven days. In Hebrew, leaven is symbolic for sin. The sinful nature of pride for instance, makes us puffed up. Therefore, it is good practice for us as well, especially during this week, to remove the leaven from our lives. Take inventory of what's in our heart. Remove anything that makes us prideful, arrogant or puffed up. God is reminding us that He hates pride.

The Feast of Passover is observed usually on the first and second day of the seven week period. Most Jewish homes will have a seder meal to commemorate this feast. A seder meal is an object lesson using different elements of food to describe how God delivered his people from slavery in Egypt, into freedom. It is important to God that we always remember. Being human, God knew we would tend to forget and take for granted what he did. Exodus 12:14 says:

> And this day shall be unto you for a memorial; and ye shall keep it a feast to the Lord throughout your generations; ye shall keep it a feast by an ordinance for ever. (KJV)

This is something God commanded us to do forever—to never stop. There is an Egypt in all of us, something that keeps us in bondage and holds us captive. We all struggle with things of this world. But as we observe Passover tonight, let's give God all of our issues. Let God break those chains that hold you back and have kept you captive. Let him set you free tonight, so that you can live a full and prosperous life.

And finally, the Feast of First Friuts, in which this feast takes place usually the day after the Passover Feast. In Egypt there was famine in the land. Famine was everywhere…except in Goshen (where the Israelites were). It did not touch them. God's hand of protection was on them. This reminds us that we may be living in this world but we are not of this world. The economy may fall and things crumble around us but God's hand of protection will sustain us. The Feast of First Fruit is a time in which the Israelites brought a sheaf of barley into the temple and presented it to the Lord. Barley was the first crop to be planted in winter and by Passover it was just beginning to ripen. This was waved before the Lord. The Lord's acceptance of the first fruit was a pledge on His part of a full harvest to come. For believers, it's a reminder that everything we have, comes from

God and that we are to bring our very best. This is part of God's blueprint for bringing prosperity to his people. It is his plan or way for us to prosper, if we will choose to obey.

God established three times a year that we are to come before him and to not come empty handed. We know that we bring our tithes and offerings. Our tithes are the ten percent of our wages, but the offerings are the three times we come before the Lord during his established feast. (I have always thought that the offerings were just what we give above and beyond our tithes), but in fact it is an offering that we give at the time of God's feast, at three different times throughout the year. When we begin to realize, God doesn't need the money, he needs your obedience, and then we will begin to reap his blessing. You cannot out give God. With whatever measure you use to bring your offering, he will use the same to repay. This is God's method or way of blessing us. You can't have a harvest without sowing seed.

> "Be not deceived; God is not mocked: for whatsoever a man soweth, that shall he also reap. Galatians 6:7 (KJV)"

2 Corinthians 9:6 also says:

> "But this I say, He which soweth sparingly shall reap also sparingly; and he which soweth bountifully shall reap also bountifully." (KJV)

God always wants your best, not the left over's. This principal applies in every area of life…sow love you get love, sow kindness you get kindness, sow hatred you get hatred.

*We will be taking up a first fruits offering a little later, so begin to think about what God would have you give. As you become familiar with the feasts from year to year, this offering should be something you plan on ahead of time and look forward to giving.**

What I have just talked about summarizes what the three feasts are all about. We are combining all three tonight.

When we say we are connected to Abraham's blessing, what is that blessing anyway? The word "bless" means the beneficial endowment of the power of God to produce well-being in every area of a person's life. The word bless contains four things: healing, prosperity, well-being for your family, and salvation for your soul. I know we all want that? So now let's look at a way to start being blessed by taking part in the remembrance of Passover entitled—A Time of Liberation

Even though God is exceedingly good and is always blessing us, there are special times—appointed times if you will—that the Lord himself made an appointment to meet with his people. These dates and times are called God's feast and holy days that he himself set as a blue print or pathway for us to follow in order to obtain his blessings and to stay free.

Let's begin with a woman of honor lighting the candles[7] and waving her hands over the lit candles three times—welcoming in God's light, health and prosperity and then praying a silent prayer. (woman lights candles)

It is appropriate that a woman bring light into the house, because it was through the woman that the light of the world, Messiah Jesus, came into the world. (read blessing together)[8]

Blessed art thou O Lord, King of the Universe, who has sanctified us in His commandments, and commanded us to kindle the Passover lights.

*If there is a Rabbi present-or someone who speaks Hebrew—they can recite the blessing in Hebrew*

## 1. At this time we will partake of the first cup, the cup of Sanctification.

We are to be a people that are set apart as sacred or holy unto God for special use or purpose. After accepting Yeshua Jesus Christ as our savior and being forgiven of sin, we start the process of *salvation; which* is a continual process

---

7    A Woman of honor lights the candles. One woman that is chosen prior to starting the Seder meal comes forward at this time to light the candles

8    Instruct everyone to read the printed blessing found at each plate aloud

of being healed, being forgiven, being made prosperous, and being made whole. He begins cleaning up our lives and setting us apart from the world for His purpose. As God begins to sanctify us…we should naturally begin to look and act different from the world. God changes us!

(Rabbi, if present says blessing in Hebrew)

*Let's all remember what God has done for us as we recite together our blessing—found in front of you on your plate

Blessed art thou our God, King of the Universe, who has preserved us alive, sustained us, and brought us to enjoy this season.

(Partake of the cup)

## 2 .Hand Washing

This is done with a large basin of water, much like a baptismal. When the apostle Peter was ask what must be done to receive the Holy Spirit, he said, …"Repent, *and be baptized* every one of you in the name of Jesus Christ for the forgiveness of your sins, *and you will* receive the gift of the Holy Spirit."(Acts 2:38 NIV). Having been saved and set apart for His purposes, we now want to be baptized and filled with the Holy Spirit. As we repent of sin and iniquities, we should wash our hands, symbolic of baptism. By washing our hands we are breaking every curse that blocks God's blessing from coming into our life and family. We are reborn by the baptism. Ephesians 5:26 KJV says: *That he might sanctify and cleanse it with the washing of water by the word.* As we wash our hands let's allow God's word to penetrate our hearts and do something spiritual in our life.

Right now we declare very curse and every family curse is broken and reversed in every area of our lives and our home.(*wash your hands in the bowl of water/ symbolic of baptism*)

## 3. The Sprig of Parsley

As you pick up the parsley, be reminded of when the Israelites were in bondage in Egypt. Many tears were shed. They were told the spirit of death was approaching. The people of Israel dipped their hyssop branches into the blood of the lamb-without spot or blemish-and applied the blood to the doorposts of their homes. As believers, we need to be applying the blood of Christ every day to our lives. Lord we need your protection——

Dip the parsley in salt water and take a bite. The salt is a representation of the bitter tears that were shed before they were delivered—as believers it represents the tears we shed "before we knew "the Son of God, the King of Kings and the Lord of Lords. Our tears were not wasted; *Psalm 56:8* says that God actually collects each tear we shed:

> "Thou tellest my wanderings; put thou my tears into thy bottle:
> are they not in thy book?" (KJV)

## 4. The Unleavened Bread

The leader of the table takes the basket or plate with the three pieces of matzah bread and removes the middle piece. The three pieces symbolizes the Father, Son, and Holy Spirit. The middle one is removed and broken. Once broken, the smaller part which represents the bread of affliction is put back inside. (This is a beautiful picture of Jesus Christ, who was taken, beaten and broken and pierced and placed in a borrowed tomb) Now in the Seder meal, the other remaining broken half (that was not put back inside) is broken up into enough pieces for each child at your table. The pieces are then wrapped in a cloth or napkin. The children are instructed to close their eyes, while the wrapped pieces are hidden around the room. After the meal, the kids are allowed to search for the hidden pieces of matzah and bring them back to receive a small prize; teaching that whomever finds Jesus Christ in this life is greatly rewarded!

(We will now have the kids to close their eyes and have one person from each table to hide the broken pieces.)

Remember the kids will find the pieces after the meal. Now this is also the part of the meal in the New Testament where Jesus broke the bread in the upper room with the disciples. He was fulfilling his promise, that his body would be broken for you and me.

*At this time we will have our pastor, (or leader) lead the church in partaking of the bread or Matzah to represent Jesus's body that was broken for us. (*we are only partaking the bread at this time*) Remember to not partake of these elements in an unworthy way—ask him to forgive you of any sin in your life.

## 5. Haggadah

The story of the Israelites exit from Egypt.

A lot of us today have traced our lineages. As believers, it is vitally important to realize where we originated. The Gentile, or non-Jew, upon receiving Jesus Christ as their Lord and savior, becomes *grafted into the family* of God. *Jesus was* Jewish. It started with the Jewish people. God established his throne to be in the city of Jerusalem. He will rule and reign from Israel. Remember he was forsaken by his own people, which opened the door for non-Jews to be saved as well. (Thank God he loved us all enough to established a plan that would save the whole world) It is not his will for any to perish.

Before we go any further, let's take a minute to bow us heads and repent for anti Semitism or hatred of the Jewish people and ask God to reverse the curse off of America, that we have brought on ourselves through hatred.

***pray***

Our story begins with Abraham becoming the first believer. God told him that he would be the father of many nations and that the world would be blessed through him. And from Abraham come Isaac and then Jacob. From Jacob we get Joseph.

Does everyone remember Joseph with the coat of many colors? His brothers were jealous of him and put him in a pit and then sold him into slavery. He ends up in Potifer's house as the second most powerful man in the world. Now there was a famine in the land and Joseph's brothers go to Egypt for food not knowing that their brother they sold was now one of the most powerful men, and in charge of the food in Egypt. And as the story goes, after he forgives them, he brings his family to Egypt, thus the children of Israel come into Egypt through Joseph. Egypt becomes very blessed because the children of God were there.

Now over the next couple hundred years God blessed the Jewish people and Egypt was being blessed as a result. But the Israelites forgot they were just to visit Egypt and not stay there. They were prospering and as years went by there came up another Pharaoh that knew them not. He did not know Joseph and his brothers. He looked at the country and saw the blessing and said we need to remove the Jewish people least they become a threat to us. He took their businesses and their herds and their flocks and made them slaves. He became so threatened that he released a decree to kill all the first born baby boys.

Now there was a mother that trusted God to protect her child. She placed him in a basket and floated him in the Nile River. The babies name was Moses. Pharaoh's daughter was bathing and found the child and took him as her own; raising him in the palace. As he grew, he saw the Jews being mistreated. He knew it wasn't right to mistreat them. Moses saw a guard hurting a Jew. He killed the guard. He then fled for his life.

While in the dessert, Moses saw a bush burning; but it was not consumed. A voice from the bush, which was the Lord, told him to go back to Pharaoh and tell him to "let my people go." Of course Moses was scared to return. But he did and every time he would ask Pharaoh; Pharaoh would say no and God would release a plaque on the land. Ten times he went. And ten plaques were released. (None of which affected the Israelites if they obeyed God)

Now a "plague of Blood" came upon the waters which were in the river, a "plague of frogs" covered the land, a "plague of gnats" came upon men and animals and all the dust became gnats, a "plague of flies" came on the people and in their houses and covering the ground, "plague on the livestock of the Egyptians"—their livestock died, a "plague of festering boils" broke out on the men and animals , a "plague of hail" destroyed their land and stripped every tree, a "plague of locusts" covered the ground and destroyed what was left, a "plague of darkness" covered all of Egypt for three days.

Each time Pharaoh refused to let them leave, yet through all this the Israelites were protected by God. The tenth plague would be a "plague on the firstborn." The Lord said about midnight I will go throughout Egypt and every firstborn son in Egypt will die. They were instructed to take a year-old male lamb without defect and slaughter them and put *the blood* on the sides and tops of the doorframes of the houses where they eat the lambs. Roast the meat over fire, along with bitter herbs, and bread made without yeast. They were to eat it before morning and burn whatever wasn't eaten.

They were to eat it with their cloak tucked into their belt and sandals on their feet and a staff in their hand, in haste. On that same night God would pass through Egypt and strike down (or kill) every firstborn—both men and animals—and he would bring judgment on all the gods of Egypt, as each plaque represented a god. The blood on the doorpost would be a sign for you on the house where you are; and when I see the blood, I will pass over you.

During the night, Pharaoh summoned Moses and Aaron and urged the people to leave in a hurry and to take their flocks and herds and go. They did as they were told and they ask for silver and gold and clothing. The Israelites were given what they ask for so they plundered the Egyptians.

## 6. This Brings Us To—The Cup of Deliverance:

As we just heard the story of God delivering his people out of bondage in Egypt, we see it was *all about the blood*. We remember the Israelites were instructed to put the blood of a spotless lamb on the sides and top of the doorframe of their houses. If they obeyed His instruction, they were spared. The Israelites were also spared the ten plaques or curses that came on the Egyptian people. God ultimately delivered them from death and destruction.

**In the Seder meal the leader dips his finger in the wine and lets it drop on the plate ten times to represent the ten plaques. (*Dip finger ten times*)

We will now recite the Blessing over the second cup together:
*Blessed art thou O Lord our God, King of the Universe, creator of the fruit of the vine.*

(Partake of the cup)

By his death on the cross, Jesus Christ became the spotless lamb, who laid down his life for mankind. Through the blood of Jesus, not only are we forgiven and free, but *free indeed*! Not only are we delivered from sin but also delivered from the curses that are linked to the sin.

The Bible says that if a man has committed a sin deserving of death, and he is put to death, and you hang him on a tree… he who is hanged is *accursed* of God. Deuteronomy 21:22-23. (NIV) And Paul says: *Galatians 3:13 Christ hath redeemed us from the curse of the law, being made a curse for us: for it is written, Cursed is everyone that hangeth on a tree:* (KJV) Jesus didn't just die for our sin—he died to break the curses or iniquity off as well. Iniquities is a bend or weakness in a person that causes them to be pulled in the direction of a negative behavior or sin. Bitterness, anger, and addiction are some of the iniquities or results from sin that people are forgiven for, but continue to wrestle with. You are not just forgiven; he gives you a brand new life- free from the curses from your past. You aren't just free but free indeed from the consequences as well.

## 7. Second Hand Washing

It reminds us that we are cleansed from the impurities and limitations of the world. It symbolizes Jesus baptism in water and because we are born again, we may be in this world, but we are not of this world. We break off the sin of this world, and like Jesus, when we come out of the water; we receive the power of the Holy Spirit. The water symbolizes divine power and wisdom.

## 8. Eating of Matzah

(The Leader pulls out the rest of the middle piece of matzah.) This represents the unleavened bread. *1 Corinthians 5:7-8 says:...For Christ, our Passover lamb, has been sacrificed. Therefore let us keep the Festival, not with the old yeast, the yeast of malice and wickedness, but with bread without yeast, the bread of sincerity and truth. (NIV)* For believers, Jesus was saying, in me, there is no leaven; in me there is no guile, no impurities of any kind. I am the unspotted, unblemished Lamb of God. (we place the bread back in the middle)

   ***Optional if a Rabbi is present*** says blessing in Hebrew

## 9. The Maror (Bitter Herbs)

(Take a pinch of bitter herbs (horseradish) and put it on a piece of Matza.)

   The bitter herbs represent how hard the Israelites were forced to work in Egypt. When you taste the horseradish it may bring tears to your eyes representing the bitterness of slavery. As believers, it should make us weep and never take for granted what Jesus endeared. Jesus was willing to be beaten, humiliated, stripped naked, and spat upon. His beard was ripped from His face. The reality of what Jesus endeared should bring tears to our eyes.

   You will also see a mixture on your plate of apples, nuts, and honey. This mixture represents the mortar the Israelites used for making bricks when they were in bondage. They were forced to work harder and harder and under unrealistic conditions. As we partake, remember the unfair conditions in which the Israelites were forced to live. Take some of the mixture and place it on the matzo and partake.

## 10. Meal of Matzah Ball Soup Served with Fruit

(servers may begin to serve the soup and fruit to the tables)

   *** Cut on festive Jewish music and give time to eat, talk and experience the food but be mindful of the time, and move things along. As people finish up, tell them you are moving on to the final part of the celebration. ***

## 11. Tzafun

(At this time, let's have the children find the pieces of matzah that were hidden around the room a little earlier. (*Give them a few minutes to search*)

The hidden matzah is ransomed back for a small gift. ***(*Give the children a small gift for finding the hidden piece*) Remember that whomever finds Jesus Christ in his life is greatly rewarded***The matzah can be eaten at the end of the meal.

## 12. Barech

"Grace" is said after the meal.

(Rabbi or speaker) Blessed is our God, from that which we eat and is His, and in His goodness we live.

## 13. Let's partake of the third cup, The cup of Redemption

This reminds us of the shed blood of the spotless, perfect, innocent Lamb. Jesus Christ became the ultimate perfect sacrifice; the Lamb that brought our redemption. We see that Jesus took the third cup in Luke 22:20 and 1 Corinthians 11:25:

> "In the same way, after supper he took the cup, saying, "This is the new covenant in my blood; do this, whenever you drink it, in remembrance of me." (NIV)

It wasn't just any cup—it was redemption from slavery into freedom.
(Pastor) if you would stand and lead us in the "communion" cup
(Pastor can elaborate on this if he chooses)
***Optional for Rabbi to say blessing in Hebrew or have everyone recite blessing aloud***

*Blessed art thou O Lord our God, King of the Universe, creator of the fruit of the vine.*

## 14. Hallel

Scripture says that God inhabits our praise. Let's sing a song of praise to Him. (choose a chorus)

## 15. Cup of Hallel

The forth cup is taken. Hallel in Hebrew means "praise." We see in John 17, that Jesus took time to praise and thank the Lord at the end of the Passover Seder, his last supper. The spotless Lamb had praise on his lip as he was facing his death.

*(partake of the cup)*

(Everyone recites the blessing)

*Blessed art thou O Lord our God, King of the Universe, creator of the fruit of the vine.*

## 16. In Jewish Seders there is a cup set for Elijah

They believe he is coming to announce the arrival of Messiah. Christians believe that Yeshua Messiah has already come, but will return again. Both are looking for the return of Yeshua Messiah.

It was just before the Passover Feast, and Jesus knew it was time for him to leave this world and go to the Father. The evening meal was being served.

"So he got up from the meal, took off his his outer clothing, and wrapped a towel around his waist. After that, he poured water into a basin and began to wash his disciples' feet, drying them with the towel that he wrapped around him...."You do not realize now what I am doing, but later you will understand." ...You call me," Teacher" and "Lord" and rightly so, for that is what I am. Now that I, your Lord and Teacher, have washed your feet, you also should wash one another's feet. I have set you an example that you should do as I have done for you. I tell you the truth, no servant is greater than his master, nor is a messenger greater than the one who sent him. Now that you know these things, you will be blessed if you do them. John 13:4-17 (NIV)

**I think it is appropriate, as his disciples, that we wash each other's feet.** At this time the servers will begin to pass the water basins, pictures of water, and towels to the guest. Please keep an attitude of prayer and reverence by holding down your voices.

\* (Leader demonstrates and everyone follows) \*

Then he comforts his disciples by saying:

> "DO NOT let your hearts be troubled. Trust in God; trust also in me. In my Father's house are many rooms; if it were not so, I would have told you. I am going there to prepare a place for you. And if I go and prepare a place for you, I will come back and take you to be with me that you also may be where I am. You know the way to the place where I am going."….He says, "If you love me, you will obey what I command. And I will ask the Father, and he will give you another Counselor to be with you forever— the Spirit of truth. The world cannot him, because it neither sees him nor knows him. But you know him, for he lives with you and will be in you. I will not leave you as orphans; I will come to you. Before long, the world will not see me anymore, but you will see me. Because I live, you also will live. On that day, you will realize that I am in my Father, and you are in me, and I am in you. Whoever has my commands and obeys them, he is the one who loves me. He who loves me will be loved by my Father, and I too will love him and show myself to him." John 14: 1-21 (NIV)

So as we commemorate Passover tonight: Remember in the Old Testament Passover there were three key elements: Bitter herbs, unleavened bread, and a spotless lamb. God delivered the Israelites out of bondage and brought them into freedom. In the New Testament, Jesus became the ultimate sacrifice, the spotless Lamb that took away the sin of the world, and spared our life. Just as he brought the people out of bondage in Egypt, he has freed us from the bondage of sin. The Old Testament is a fore shadowing of the New Testament. Passover was established by God on the foundation of His blood covenant with mankind; and we are still in covenant with him today. The Passover feast is a part of our spiritual heritage and reminds us of how He set us free. Passover literally means "protection", and it comes from the instructions given by God to those marked with blood. God says in Exodus 12:24:

> "And ye shall observe this thing for an ordinance to thee and to thy sons for ever." (KJV)

Like the early church of the New Testament believers, if we do this, it *releases* great blessing and benefits into our lives! Through the blood of Jesus Christ this Passover season and your obedience to align yourself with God, We release *seven* specific supernatural blessings for your body, your family, your finances, and your future. As we read in Exodus 23[9], in honoring God during Passover, He will:

1. Assign an angel to you
2. Be an enemy to your enemies
3. Give you prosperity
4. Take sickness away from you
5. Give you a long life
6. Bring increase and inheritance
7. Give a special year of blessing

***If you have a first fruits offering—at this time you can come to bring it and place it in the basket** as we keep an attitude of reverence.... find a quiet place to pray and seek God. You are welcome to stay as long as you want, but this will conclude our service. ***

"Watch therefore, for you do not know what hour your Lord is coming. Do you realize that next year, we could be celebrating Passover with the Lamb Himself?

(Soft music is played in the background during prayer time.)

---

9   Refer to Exodus 23 (CEV)

# The Feast of Pentecost/ Shavout Preparation List

1.  I like to put two tables together to accommodate seating for twelve people per table. (Tables can be placed any way you like) I use disposable white paper table clothes. Decorate tables for a harvest look, using lots of greenery branches and flowers. I used clay pots and baskets. Each was filled with herbs and vegetables and loaves of wheat and barley. I used votive candles for decoration. Tables can be decorated as nice or kept as simple as you like.

2.  Each table should have treys containing the seven items: wheat, barley, olives, dates, figs, pomegranates, and grapes. (Or prepare dishes made from these, such as grape salad, cookies made with fig, etc.) It is not necessary to include all seven items but I like to use it as a point of teaching)

3.  Each table should have treys containing **cheese cake** (I used the sample cheese cake squares from Sam's)

4.  Several **loaves of wheat bread** are used at each table with **individual plastic cups of herbs mixed with olive oil and vinegar** for dipping the bread. (Premixed spices are good to use, or make your own combination

5. Each guest should be given a **copy of the Ten Commandments** and a sheet that compares the Old Testament and the New Testament. Place these at each place setting.

6. The table should be complete with a **plate, silverware, cup and napkin** in each place setting. (I used the clear plastic plates, etc. to look nice, but conveniently thrown away) with paper doilies.

7. Have **a basket in which to place the offerings.**

8. **A basket of herbs** to hand out as a gift. (I used sprigs from three different herbs and bound them together with twine or ribbon to be passed out to individual guest. The herbs give off a wonderful aroma and will be a continual reminder during the coming week of this season of harvest.)

9. Treys and food should be prepared prior to the celebration and ready to serve. Servers should be ready to help distribute food to the guest at the appropriate times.

10. **Tea, water and coffee** are the only beverages served, to keep things simple; but one could use whatever beverage they choose. You can go to as much trouble as you like, or keep it as simple as you like.

11. You can **serve a main dish** if you want-pasta with chicken is a good idea and can be refrigerated the night before. Cheese dip placed in hollowed out bread is an idea. Cheese balls are something that can be prepared the night before. All of these ideas are primarily made with milk; just get creative. See the internet for food ideas for Pentecost Feast.

## Other Suggestive Ways to Celebrate Pentecost

1. Always review what God says in his word about Pentecost and its meaning, but in addition:

2. Read and remember the Ten Commandments

3. Read the book of Ruth. It teaches loyalty, love and being tolerant.

4. Prepare a meal. During Pentecost, we can eat almost anything we like. But always dairy since this reminded them that once they received the Torah, they were like babies who only drink milk.

5. Blintzes or cheese kreplach-dumplings, Jewish crepes, or cheesecake are commonly seen on Jewish tables.

6. Always be prepared to give your second "first fruit offering." Remember to always plan ahead of time for these offerings, as this is a window of opportunity that only passes by once a year.

# Pentecost: The End of Bondage and the Beginning of God`s Covenant Blessing

## (Script for Leader)

> "I was glad when they said unto me Let us go into the house of the Lord." Psalm 122:1 (KJV)

HAS ANYONE EVER READ THIS in the Bible? It was during the time of the Feast of Shavuot or should I say Pentecost. The people were filled with joy, excitement, and anticipation awaiting the time of the festival. My hope is that as we glean information about God's feast, we too will become so excited about our appointments with God that we will look forward to these times and plan ahead. These are dates that God himself arranged with mankind—we don't want to miss them.

There are three Hebrew words used in the Scriptures about the Feast of God. The first word is "moed", which means appointment, set time, cycle, or assembly. The second word is "miqra" which means convocation or rehearsal. The third word is "chag" which means feast, to move in a circle, dance, celebration, and rejoicing. So from these words, we can see the Feast of the Lord are sacred assemblies or convocations of God's people at appointed times to rehearse what God has done in the past and will do in the future through the Messiah, to save mankind. Genesis 1:14 says:

"And God said, Let there be lights in the firmament of the heavens to divide the day from the night; and let them be for signs, and for seasons, and for days, and years" (KJV)

The word seasons in Genesis 1:14 in the hebrew is moed. Moed means appointment or fixed time. This word indicates the cycle of the phases of the moon to help people know the festivals and harvest and appointed times. It is not referring to the four seasons, summer, autumn, winter, spring. This is referring to God's feasts or appointed times. God gave us a blueprint to follow. It is to show us how to live and to be prosperous and blessed and to have the abundance he intended for us. These feast of the Lord belong to all those who believe in Him.

Remember the first appointed feast of God was the Feast of Passover, which was the New Year for Israel. At Passover, we also celebrated the Feast of Unleavened Bread and the Feast of First Fruits. These feast brought the favor of God. Tonight we are celebrating the Feast of Pentecost ushering in the prosperity of God. I believe we all want to be prosperous.

Fifty is a significant number associated with the Feast of Pentecost. It had been exactly *fifty days* from when God set his people free from bondage in Egypt when he gave them the Ten Commandments, thus the first Pentecost in the Old Testament. Then looking ahead in the New Testament, Jesus died on the cross and *exactly fifty days* later, he gave them the Holy Spirit, at Pentecost. Fifty refers to a time of Jubilee, when every fifty years God set the people free, cancelled all their debt, and brought the new harvest. Jubilee, for us today, represents a time in which God restores everything we have lost, rejected, or missed out on. Jubilee refers to a time of double blessing. What a truly exciting time, when we are not only blessed but receive a double blessing.

In the Old Testament we remember the Israelites were in bondage in Egypt and being abused and forced to work. God heard the cry of his people by causing Pharaoh to allow them to leave Egypt, thus setting them free. Although set free, they were clueless as to what to do to stay free. God never leaves us in the wilderness. He will always take us to a higher place.

Therefore he established a system to bless his people. It was a time to enter into a covenant with God, a time for God to connect his promises to our lives. God has established appointed times in the Bible. The Lord's Feast is appointments made by God himself at certain times throughout the whole year. These times were seed times to sow seed if you wanted optimal blessings. They learned the principal of sowing and reaping in Gen. 1:11.

> "And God said, Let the earth bring forth grass, the herb yielding seed, and the fruit tree yielding fruit after his kind, whose seed is in itself, upon the earth: and it was so." (KJV)

It teaches that every seed produces after its own kind. *Be not deceived; God is not mocked: for whatsoever a man soweth, that shall he also reap. Galatians 6:7 (KJV)* God always does things in the spiritual and in the natural. For instance, if you sow an apple seed, you get an apple; you *never* sow an apple seed and harvest an orange. Just like in the spiritual sense, if you sow love, you get love. Sow forgiveness, and you get forgiven. If you sow bitterness, you become bitter. But, one thing is certain, if a farmer does not sow *any* seed, he cannot expect *any* harvest. The Bible also teaches to sow on good soil. There are optimal times for sowing and specific seasons to sow certain crops. For instance, to enjoy certain flowers in the spring—you must plant the bulbs in the fall. In Deuteronomy 16, God say "there are three times to come before me and to not come empty handed;" this is at the Feast of Passover, at the Feast of Pentecost, and at the Feast of Trumpets. The Bible talks of tithes and offerings. We were taught to tithe our first ten percent of what we make. I have always thought that offerings were anything above and beyond that. Our offerings are actually the three times a year God said to come before him and not to come empty handed. We have just celebrated Passover, in which we bring our first, first fruit offering before the Lord. The Hebrew word for first fruits is "bikkurim", and means a promise to come or firstborn. As we honor God with this offering; he *promises* a fresh outpouring of wisdom, favor, anointing and prosperity. Counting fifty days after the first fruit offering at Passover, brings us to Shavuot or Pentecost, in which we are to sow our second first fruit offering as we see in Lev 23:15-16:

> "And ye shall count unto you from the morrow after the sabbath, from the day that ye brought the sheaf of the wave offering; seven sabbaths shall be complete: Even unto the morrow after the seven Sabbath shall ye number fifty days; and ye shall offer a new meat offering unto the Lord." (KJV)

Shavuot or the Feast of Weeks (also known as Pentecost) is the feast of the Lord that is celebrated on the fiftieth day after the Feast of First Fruits.

Pentecost, or Shavuot, first of all is a harvest feast, celebrating the ingathering of the first harvest. Does anyone remember at the Passover Feast, the first crop in season during Passover? (barley) They brought offerings of barley before the Lord. Now the harvest has reached its fullness and is ready and they have gathered their crops. During Pentecost, in Temple times, the people would bring two loaves of wheat bread made with yeast from the first fruit of the wheat harvest. They would waive the two loaves before the Lord as a gesture of Thanksgiving. The High Priest would lift up the two loaves before the Lord to symbolize the coming abundance and the miracle harvest that was promised during this season. The two leaven loaves have a meaning. Does anyone know what the meaning is? It is symbolic of sinful mankind—both Jew and Gentile or non-Jew. (Remember they are made with yeast and yeast puffs things up and is symbolic of sin—and there are two loaves-Jew and non-Jew) The message was one of prosperity, anointing and God's wisdom being released into our lives.

Another interesting bit of information about Pentecost is that it brings the entire *spring* Feast to an end. Pentecost represents the final Feast connected with Yeshua's *first* coming, (God's word speaks of his first and second coming) bringing it to a full completion. Remember we have already observed Passover, First Fruits, and Unleavened Bread. We now arrive at Pentecost. The remaining Feast of the Lord all occur together four months later, and are linked to Yeshua's *second* coming.

So let's talk about Shavuot. After the Jews left Egypt they camped in the Sinai desert opposite Mount Sinai. Moses was told by God to gather the Israelites together to receive the Torah, or path/ guideline. God instructed Moses to tell the people to prepare themselves. *(Exodus 19:14 KJV)* For three days before he was to give them instructions, they were to sanctify themselves, wash their clothes and not have relations with their spouses. (This is still good practice for us to follow as it helps us to be prepared to encounter and hear from our Holy God tonight) But God required them to be clean before them. Their response was: *And all the people answered together, and said, All that the LORD has spoken we will do. And Moses returned the word of the people unto the LORD*[10]. after preparing, they were told to come near. Dense clouds covered the peak or top of the mountain. Thunder and lightning were seen and heard. The sound of the shofar came very strong and the mountain top was consumed in fire and smoke. The Israelites were in amazement. Moses went up the mountain alone and a mighty voice announced the Ten Commandments. The Torah or guideline that was given represented the word of God, the Bible. Torah, commonly translated in English, is law. *But in Hebrew*, Torah means instruction or teaching (not Law). Therefore, it should be understood that the law or Torah (which was the first five books of the Old Testament) was God's instruction manual for teaching us, so that we could understand him better and to give us a good, long life. The law is not a list of do's and don'ts, as we generally think; but instructions for a blessed, long life. And the Torah was given exactly fifty days from the crossing of the Red Sea. In other words, He brought them out of bondage and fifty days later He gave them instruction on how to have a good long life and remain free from bondage. Pentecost is called the season of the giving of the Torah in Hebrew because this is the literal day that God revealed himself to the people as they stood at the base of the mountain.

Let's look at some comparisons of Pentecost in the Old Testament and in the New Testament:[11]

---

10  Exodus 19:8 (KJV)

11  Refer to Sheet/Handout.

Pentecost is also seen as a marriage or betrothal contract. The beautiful image is that of the marriage between God (the Groom) and Israel (the bride). There are two stages to a wedding as seen in God's word. The first stage, was the betrothal, called erusin in Hebrew. You enter the first stage of marriage as soon as the written contract is made between two parties. This is called a ketubah. At this point you are legally married but do not physically live with the mate. It is a very binding contract that one cannot get out of without a get, or divorce contract. The second stage of the marriage is the fullness or consummation of the marriage (KJV) shows us that at Mount Sinai, God betrothed Himself to Israel. And in Exodus 19 (KJV), God brought the Israelites to Mt. Sinai, he betrothed himself to her and gave the Torah to her. He was making a ketubah or written contract with her. This contact spelled out mutual obligations of God and Israel just as a husband and a wife would do. So God made a marriage contract with Israel. Israel accepts the contract in Exodus 19:8 (KJV). It says Israel camped before the Lord. The word camp in Hebrew is chanah, and is singular in this context, while Israel is plural. By this we see that all Israel had become one. This is also a necessary requirement for marriage. The wedding was to be consummated under a wedding canopy known as a chuppah. In Exodus 19:17[12] (KJV) Moses brought the people to meet God and they stood at the nether part of the mount. Nether in Hebrew actually implies that the people stood underneath the mountain, giving us a wonderful image that the mountain became a chupah and the people were standing underneath the mountain where the wedding took place. A wedding has two witnesses present to sign the ketubah. Moses was one witness but he did not sign the two tablets. When he saw Israel worshiping the golden calf, he knew they were violating the covenant and being unfaithful in their marriage, and he broke the tablets. Because of this, Israel did not enter into the full marriage. Yeshua is the groom and the believers in Messiah are betrothed to Him. He came so that whosoever

---

12 Exodus 19:17-Moses led them out of the camp to meet God, and they stood at the foot of the mountain (CEV)

would put their trust in Him would be married to him forever, Jew and non-Jews. We are now spiritually betrothed to him. But one day we will be spiritually and physically married to him in the Millennium. After the honeymoon in heaven, Yeshua will be returning with his bride to attend the marriage supper. We are going to rule and reign with him physically forever. What an awesome time that is going to be!

## Explain table decoration

Let's look at our table and think about what was going on during the time of Shavuot.

In preparation for the pilgrimage to Jerusalem to celebrate Shavuot or Pentecost, farmers prepared their crops and tied red threads around any fig, pomegranate or grapes that were ripe. They also brought wheat; barley, olives, and dates piled in baskets and carried them in procession to Jerusalem. Leading the procession was a flutist and an ox, with its horns painted gold. It mattered not whether one was rich and poor; they all came to the festival with great joy. This was such a fun and exciting time for everyone. Half of the day was used in studying and learning while the other half of the day, they were eating. Each family would carry a basket full of their first fruits to the Temple in Jerusalem. Their basket would be filled with Israel's seven fruits that were mentioned in Deuteronomy 8:8 (KJV), where it talked of a land of wheat and barley and vines and fig and pomegranates and a land of olive oil and (dates) honey.

The day of Pentecost was a time of thanksgiving and happiness. Synagogues were decorated with beautiful greenery branches and flowers, as the harvest had come in and everything had reached its fullness. Some put grass on the floor to symbolize the grass on which the Israelites stood as they received the Torah. Sometimes sweet smelling herbs and grasses would be given out at the services.

***Our helpers are now going to hand out sweet smelling gifts** for you to take home. As you smell this bouquet of herbs, let it be a reminder for the next few days of this festive, joyful time that God came into a marriage covenant with us and gave us the commandments, so that we could live a long prosperous life full of blessing.

**We are now going to enjoy some delicious food and fellowship** as I will explain how it relates to our feast.

***My helpers are now going to serve you.

*First they are bringing a tray of cheesecake.** Why do we eat cheesecake at this time? It is a reminder of when God gave Moses the Ten Commandments. To the Israelites, it was like a baby beginning to drink milk. A baby has to work up to eating meat. They too stared out drinking the milk of the word; then progressed on to the meat of the word. So at Shavuot or Pentecost, we like to eat things that are made primarily from milk. As believers we do the same thing by starting out with the milk of the word and working up to the meat. Let me remind you: we can't always remain babies; we have to mature in the Lord.

*You also see on our table loaves of wheat bread**. This reminds us of the two loaves that represented sinful mankind, both the Jew and non-Jew. Remember at Shavuot, they would waive the two loaves before the Lord as a gesture of Thanksgiving. The High Priest would lift up the two loaves before the Lord to symbolize the coming abundance and the miracle harvest promised during the season. So let's enjoy some bread dipped in oil and spices. You will find bowls of spices on the table. Stir the spices and oil up to amalgamate the flavor, and break a piece of bread off and dip it into the mixture.

*Remember we said that there were **seven fruits** that were mentioned in Deuteronomy 8:8 (KJV). This verse talked of a land of wheat and barley and vines and figs and pomegranates and a land of olive oil and dates and honey. We will be bringing these items, or things made from these items, to your table for you to sample and try.

***(Turn on Jewish festive music and enjoy the food but be mindful not to spend too much time here. Other foods can be added to the menu depending on how elaborate or simple you want your feast to be.)

I hope you enjoyed the food and fellowship. Let's continue with the second part of our feast. Pentecost was more than just being set free; it was God's strategy or blueprint for staying free. Our covenant with the Lord is more than just being brought of out of Egypt: it includes a journey of spiritual and financial prosperity to the promise land to receive the power, revelation and blessing of God. Pentecost symbolizes two main things. It's the end of bondage and the beginning of a journey of new opportunities and a new start. It's the beginning of God's covenant blessing being released in your life. There are fifty days connecting Passover to Pentecost. This means you are coming out of the land of not enough and into the land of more than enough. God told Moses to tell the people:

(Reader #1) **Then you shall keep the Feast of Weeks to the LORD your God with the tribute of a freewill offering from your hand, which you shall give as the LORD your God blesses you. And you shall rejoice before the LORD your God, you and your son and your daughter, your male servant and your female servant, the Levite who is within your towns, the sojourner, the fatherless, and the widow who are among you, at the place where the LORD your God will choose, to make His name dwell there. Deuteronomy 16:10-11 (ESV)

You have to sow a seed to get a harvest. God told us to observe Pentecost with a free-will or first fruit offering not so He can *get* something from us. But so He *can give* something *to us*. If you sow a seed offering, God wants to *give* you the harvest. God wants us living in prosperity, blessing, abundance, and overflow. We will be giving our first fruit offering to God later on in the feast.

As I have said before, the Old Testament is a foreshadowing of the New Testament. The power of the Holy Spirit was poured out on the first church in Jerusalem on the *first* Pentecost in the Old Testament which was on Mount Sinai. Here God spoke to Moses and gave Israel and the whole world the Torah or guidelines for how to live. Remember the Israelites came out of bondage from Egypt and fifty days later, God gave Moses the Ten Commandments at Mt. Sinai. These commandments were written on two stones. This was the actual words and wisdom of God himself. Now I think we are all familiar with the Ten Commandments.

Let's look at the list of **Ten Commandments** in front of you and repeat them together:

*(Look at list—can pick a person to lead and repeat the commandments together)*

In contrast, four thousand years later, we know that Jesus, the Messiah came and died on the cross and rose from the dead to remove the bondage and slavery of *sin* from our lives. (Just as he brought the Israelites out of slavery and bondage in the Old Testament, He brought us out of slavery and bondage in the New Testament as well) Then fifty days later, when the day of Pentecost was fully come, something very wonderful happened. Let me tell you about the events:

Jesus had died on the cross and had risen from the dead. Acts 1 tells us Jesus, through the Holy Ghost, showed his chosen apostles, that he was *alive*. (He had risen just as he said) He gave them commandments and began to teach.

> "And being assembled together with them, commanded them that they should not depart from Jerusalem, but wait for the promise of the Father, which, saith he, ye have heard of me. For John truly baptized with water; but ye shall be baptized with the Holy Ghost not many days hence. Acts 1:4-5" (SKJV)

Let's rethink what we said earlier: remember, Shavuot or Pentecost, as we were talking about at the beginning, was a time when people from every part of the country would be making their way to Jerusalem to celebrate the Harvest Feast known as Shavuot. They would come and camp out around Jerusalem counting down the days until Pentecost. This was called counting the Omer. The disciples were also there. When they arrived, they went upstairs to the room where they were staying, and all joined together constantly praying, along with the women and Mary, the mother of Jesus, and with his brothers [Acts 1:13-14][13] (ERV) They were "counting the Omer" before the Lord in the Upper Room, or should I say, counting the last ten decisive days, waiting for the Feast of Shavuot to come. It is customary, even today for Jews to be up all night from Shavuot evening until the next morning on the day of Shavuot, watching in prayer and study of the word.

***A shofar (or an instrument that sounded similar to a trumpet) would be blown. *(if you have someone that can blow a shofar at this time—do so)* And the leader of their group would yell, *"get up, get up* let us go to Zion." The people would get ready and were excited and very joyful. *"I was glad when they said unto me, Let us go into the house of the Lord. Psalms122: 1 (KJV)" They* were talking about the Feast. They were filled with joy and expectancy because they knew it was time for them to bring their offering. It was time for God to open the windows of heaven and pour them out a blessing, a double portion. Let me say too, they realized this was a window of opportunity that was passing by that would not come again until the next year. You see, God blesses us all year but there are appointed times that God wants to specifically pour us out a blessing that we cannot contain. An example was when Jesus was passing through the city and the beggars were at the gate. He did not come through that city again. This was a one time opportunity. Jesus had more than enough power to heal all of them, but only one man acted out on his faith and was healed. There is a window of opportunity that is passing by right now, this day, this very night. But, are we going to seize the moment and call out to the Lord as He is passing

---

13   When they entered the city, they went to the upstairs room where they were staying. These are the ones who were there: Peter, John, James, Andrew, Philip, Thomas, Bartholomew, Matthew, James (the son of Alphaeus), Simon, the Zealot, and Judas (the son of James). The apostles were all together. They were constantly praying with the same purpose. Some women, Mary the mother of Jesus, and his brothers were there with the apostles. Acts 1:13-14 ERV

by or are we going to let this opportunity pass. The Bible says: *My people* perish, for lack of knowledge.

So we see they had all come together in one accord, waiting and praying (counting the Omer) as the disciples were also in the upper room in one accord waiting, when something extraordinary, something outrageous, something so awesome and wonderful and exciting happened! Let's listen

***Reader #2 Acts 2:1-21 (TMB) And when the day of Pentecost was fully come, they were all with one accord in one place. And suddenly there came a sound from heaven as of a rushing mighty wind, and it filled all the house where they were sitting. And there appeared unto them cloven tongues like as of fire, and it sat upon each of them. And they were all filled with the Holy Ghost, and began to speak with other tongues, as the Spirit gave them utterance. And there were dwelling at Jerusalem Jews, devout men, out of every nation under heaven. Now when this was noised abroad, the multitude came together, and was confounded, because that every man heard them speak in his own language. And they were all amazed and marveled, saying one to another, Behold, are not all these which speak Galileans? And how hear we every man in our own tongue, wherein we were born?

(Then skip down to verse 12) And they were all amazed, and were in doubt, saying one to another. What meanest this? Others mocking said, these men are full of new wine. But Peter, standing up with the eleven, lifted up his voice, and said unto them. Ye men of Judaea, and all ye that dwell at Jerusalem, be this known unto you, and hearken to my words. For these are not drunken, as ye suppose, seeing it is but the third hour of the day. But this is that which was spoken by the prophet Joel; And it shall come to pass in the last days, saith God, I will pour out of my Spirit upon all flesh: and your sons and your daughters shall prophesy, and your young men shall see visions, and your old men shall dream dreams: And on my servants and on my handmaidens I will pour out in those days of my Spirit: and they shall prophesy: And I will show wonders in heaven above, and signs in the earth beneath: blood, and fire, and vapor of smoke: The sun shall be turned into darkness, and the moon into blood, before that great and notable day of the Lord come: And it shall come to pass that whosoever shall call on the name of the Lord shall be saved.

So we see God baptized them with the Holy Ghost. He did not say to them—I have something for you—IF you want it. He *commanded* them *not to leave* until they received the Holy Ghost. This was not an option. They needed this to be equipped to go out and win the world. You see the Holy Spirit is so much more. The Bible says the Holy Spirit is the *Spirit of Truth*—think about it. It is the very all knowing wisdom of God. Don't we all need that in making decisions and in discerning right from wrong? You see God knows that there are a lot of voices in this world, and we have to know the right one to listen to, to live a prosperous and victorious life. The Holy Spirit is the *very same power or spirit* that raised Jesus from the dead. It is the boldness that rises up inside of you and causes you to stand up for what's right or to witness in this world….. But, it is also that stirring, deep down inside that starts to well up like the currents of an ocean until you are overcome with waves of love and an indescribable feeling like no other— that makes you never want to leave His presence! There's absolutely no substitute for the Holy Spirit that can comfort, satisfy, fulfill and complete you like He can. That's why before he died on the cross he told his disciples it was *imperative that he go*. He told the disciples, "I have to go, but I'm going to send a comforter." You see as long as Jesus was present on earth, he was in human form, and could only be *in one place at a time*. But after Jesus Christ died, he sent the Holy Spirit on Pentecost, and is now *omnipresent* in every believer. He is now present with you everywhere you go. He is not in just human form like before, in one place, but omnipresent; he is with you always. Do you get that? He died for your sins, and *broke the curse of your sins*, because of his death *on the cross*. Therefore, you can get free from the bondage of sin that was brought into your life. Now Jesus Christ is living inside and working through every believer to accomplish the purpose he created you for at conception. Wow, what a plan!

Looking at the Old Testament Pentecost and the New Testament Pentecost, there are similarities:

*** (*You can look at the similarities on the handout*)

We read in Acts, in the New Testament about the fire and a strong sound from heaven that was heard all over, very much like it was on Mount Sinai in the Old Testament, when the Torah was given."On the morning of the third day there was thunder and lightning with a thick cloud over the mountain, and a very loud trumpet blast. Everyone in the camp trembled. Then Moses led the people out of the camp to meet with God, and they stood at the foot of the mountain. Mount Sinai was covered with smoke, because the Lord descended on it in fire. (*In what? fire*)

> The smoke billowed up from it like smoke from a furnace, the whole mountain trembled violently." Exodus 19:16-18 (KJV)

In the New Testament, Pentecost was when the Spirit of God wrote the Torah (or laws) on the hearts of the disciples, according to the promise of the Father in Ezekiel 36:27:

> "And I will put my Spirit within you, and cause you to walk in my statutes, and you shall keep my judgments, and do them."(KJV)

> In the same way the Torah was written by the finger of God on tablets of stone in the Old Testament at Mt. Sinai, the finger of God is an expression for the Spirit of God in Matthew 12:28 and Luke 11:20, When the Lord finished speaking to Moses on Mount Sinai, he gave him the two tablets of the Testimony, the tablets of stone inscribed by the finger of God. Exodus 31:18

Pentecost as described in the Old Testament is a harvest Feast, the ingathering of the first harvest. In the New Testament, as a result of the infilling of the Holy Spirit on the day of Pentecost, three thousand people were born again that same day. It was the first harvest unto the Lord. *Then they that gladly received his word were baptized: and the same day there were added unto them about three thousand souls. Acts 2:41 (KJV)*

We need to realize that God wants to do the same mighty work in us today as he did on Pentecost. We need to realize that our salvation experience is not complete until the Spirit of God has filled us. His purpose is to make us righteous in Him by writing his laws on our heart. This feast is about the marriage union between our God and his people. We need to stay connected to Him and in covenant with Him!

Since we know now, that Pentecost is one of the appointed times we are to bring an offering before the Lord, and not to come empty handed, I am going to give anyone who would like, an opportunity to present an offering to the Lord at this time. Begin to prepare your gift. We are going to take it before the Lord in an act of obedience. I will give you a couple of minutes to prepare. We are going to resume the final part of the service in the sanctuary.

## In sanctuary

*(Distribute the Readings Handout)*

We are told to go to the place with a basket where the Lord chooses to place His name,

We are told to go to the priest—so at this time I will ask the Pastor (*or Priest*) to come forward. (*Pastor comes forward with readings*)

*(**Pastor**) If there is anyone who desires to give an offering please come forward at this time and place it in the basket. (Have the basket ready)

*(**Pastor**) let us make our confession

*(**Everyone**) I confess this day unto the Lord thy God that I have come unto the country which the Lord swore unto our fathers (Abraham, Isaac, and Jacob) to give us.

*(**Pastor**) I will set this offering before the Lord. Let us say before the Lord our God

*(**Everyone**) We praise the Lord for all the things that Jesus Christ has brought us through. You are taking us out of slavery and bringing us into the land that God promised in the Abrahamic Covenant

\*(**Pastor**) Right now as we confess to the Lord what he has done for us and delivered us from, we are recognizing and acknowledging with our profession combined with our first fruit offering that Jehovah God is the source of everything we have. God not only gives; He also sustains and keeps us. And as we do this and bring our offering, we are actually setting this before the Lord. "*we set it.*" Take a few minutes to confess to God what he has done for you in your life.

(Take a few minutes)

\*(**Pastor**) Look down on us and bless your people, and the land which thou hast given, as thou swarest unto our fathers, a land that floweth with milk and honey. This day the Lord thy God commanded thee to do these statutes and judgments: thou shalt therefore keep and do them with all thine heart, and with all thy soul. You have asked the Lord this day to be thy God, and to walk in his ways, and to keep his statutes, and his commandments, and his judgments, and to hearken unto his voice: And the Lord hath avouched thee this day to be his peculiar people, as he hath promised thee, and thou shouldest keep all his commandments: And to make thee high above all nations which he hath made, in praise, and in name, and in honor; and that thou mayest be an holy people unto the Lord thy God, as he hath spoken.

Now as we have been obedient and acted upon His word, our God is obligated based on the Abrahamic Covenant, to see us through.

\*(**Pastor**) If I could have everyone come forward and stand together.

I will anoint everyone's hands for prosperity. (*Anoint everyone's hands at one time—then pray*)

I will lay hands on everyone's forehead for wisdom and the gifts of the Holy Spirit. (*Anoint everyone's forehead at one time, and say a corporate prayer that all curses are broken off our lives and that all debt is cancelled.*)

Just spend time with God, as this will be the closure of our Feast tonight.

(Prayer can continue as long as desired—just keep an attitude of worship and reverence)

# Rosh Hashanah/Feast of Trumpets Preparation List

## Setting Up The Tables

1. I like to use a reception hall that is near a kitchen if possible

2. **Blowing of the shofar** (if you don't have anyone that plays the shofar or a trumpet, you can substitute by finding a cd of Jewish music that generally has the blowing of the shofar and pause it in place). I like to have **Messianic Jewish music playing** as people are arriving, and while eating; and soft Jewish music playing in background during prayer time.

3. A **demonstration table** is set up and decorated in the front for the leader in charge of the feast. (I like to decorate with an arrangement of flowers, something with a trumpet, baskets, etc.

4. **Two candles in candle holders** are set at the front table with matches (pick a *lady* prior to starting that will come up and light the candles) explain to her that she will wave her hands over the lit candles three times and then place her hands over her eyes and say a silent prayer. This can be for whatever is on her mind. If no

woman is present, a man may light the candle. Explanation for the lightening of the candles is in the script. I set the shofar on this table.

5.   Copies of the **recited blessings** are placed at each place setting.

6.   A cup of **grape juice/wine** is placed at the demonstration table and at each place setting.

7.   Two eight foot tables are put together to make one large table to accommodate twelve people. The number of people you are planning for will determine the number of tables you will need. Single tables can be used if desired. These are just suggestions.

8.   Nice white paper table clothes (these look nice but are disposable and do not have to be cleaned) One can use tablecloths printed with fall decorations on them if you choose.

9.   **Clear plastic plates, cups for beverage, napkins, and fork, knife and spoon** at each place setting. I like to use the clear plastic items with the clear plastic wine glasses for the wine/ grape juice, because it looks nice. But other suggestions are communion cups or just regular disposable cups. (Communion cups work well for the wine/juice)You can make it as nice or elaborate as you want.

10.  I do not place the food on the table until the appropriate time, so as not to be a distraction or temptation until it is time to eat

11.  I *do* allow guest to get their beverage as they are being seated.

12.  **Treys will be served with individual cups of honey for each guest.**—Two small treys of apple slices per table to share (for dipping in honey)

13.  **Two small loaves of classic apple honey cake** are placed on each table (can find recipes on line or simply find your own recipes to fit the feast.

14. **One loaf of Challah bread** baked in a circle is placed on each table (Harris Teeter grocery store usually carries)

15. **A trey of mini sweet potato muffins** is placed on each table. (Have also used sweet potato casserole) Search for a dish made from sweet potato.

16. **A trey of Pomegranate** is served (sometimes the seeds can only be found because it is not always in season) If nothing else—I serve one hundred percent pomegranate juice and explain the composition of a pomegranate and how it is filled with many, many seeds (as seen in script). Some other ideas or dishes made with pomegranate are jelly or chocolate covered pomegranate.

17. Small individual cups of **salad with carrot** on top are served (or some kind of carrot dish can be substituted) example: carrot cake

18. Two treys per table of **Salmon dip with sea salt crackers** are placed on each table. Some other type of fish dish can be substituted. Some Jewish families place the head of a fish on the table (but this can cause a strong fishy smell. For this reason, I do not use a fishes head but will explain the reason for the fish as seen in the script)

19. One or more **readers** are selected prior to starting and are given a copy of the verses, so they will be ready to read when called upon. This breaks things up and gets others involved.

20. I like to set up a *small* **swimming pool**. (With real fish if possible, but not necessary) You could use any small body of water. Place a bowl of **bread crumbs** beside the pool to be used later at the end of the service. One could also decorate using beta fish center pieces at each table. (This is just another option)

# A New Year/A New Beginning: Celebrating Rosh Hashanah/The Feast of Trumpets

**(Script for Leader)**

*BLOW THE SHOFAR*

"Welcome, and may you be inscribed in the Book of Life and sealed for a good year."

You see, this is one way you may be greeted and blessed by our Jewish friends during this time. So, I would like to just take this time to say welcome and greetings to you.

At this time, we will ask** (*woman that was selected prior to starting*) **to come forward and light the candles. (*Matches on table*)

When a woman lights the candles, it reminds us that every since Eve, women promote peace and unity. It was a woman that gave birth to Jesus Christ, the very light of the world. The woman is very special to God. One candle represents peace and the other blessing. This reminds us that no matter where we are, or how dark it is around us, when God is present in your life there is always light. She waives her hands over the light three times, ushering in God's light, prosperity, and health into our lives.

Now let's recite together the blessing* (your blessing is on the paper located in your plate) **

**\*\*Blessed are you Lord, Our God, King of the Universe, who creates the Fruit of the Vine\*\***

\*Let's all drink the cup of juice together

The juice or wine is a symbol of joy. It was the first miracle Jesus preformed at the wedding by turning the water into wine. Nehemiah 8:10 says

"...for the joy of the Lord is your strength." (KJV)

Let's declare today that we are going to bind and prevent every spirit that would try to steal or take away our joy. Let's also pray God's blessing over our service. I pray that He will open our eyes to see clearly his plan and open our ears to hear what his word is saying to us.

\*Let's take a minute to pray

The sound you heard at the beginning of our Feast was the sound of the shofar, or as some may say the trumpet. Tonight's feast is the Feast of Trumpets, or Rosh Hashanah. God declares the blowing of the shofar as mandatory for this Feast. So what exactly is a shofar? The shofar is made from a hollowed out ram's horn; and is the world's oldest wind instrument. Its sound is primitive and piercing and is a wakeup call to repentance. It is intended to cause believers to wake up and get their lives in order and get reconnected to God. The blowing of the shofar heralds the beginning of the period known as "The High Holy Days." The High Holy Days are the most widely observed of all of the feast times.

This is a very serious time on God's calendar that should not be taken lightly. When you hear the blowing of the shofar during the feast of trumpets, it should cause you to take inventory of your life. It is a time of reflection and repentance and restoring broken relationships. The blowing of the shofar awakens our spirit, and actually forces the enemy back. Let's think about what happens when the shofar is blown. First, breath is taken into the horn. Breath in Hebrew is the same word used for spirit. God breathed the breath of life into mankind. He breathed part of himself in us. When his spirit came into us—we became a living being. He came face to face with us. (This is likened to CPR) Remember he spoke the animals into existence but he actually breathed "himself" into mankind—and we became a living, breathing, being. There is a big difference. So as breath or His spirit is pushed in, a blessing is going out.

The Feast of Trumpets, the feast we are celebrating tonight, actually began thirty days prior. The thirty days leading up to the Feast of Trumpets, is known as the month of Elul. This is a time spent soul searching. God always gives us fair warning. God wants us to search our heart for hidden areas of unforgiveness, hurt and bitterness. Have you wronged someone? Or has someone wronged you? Have you done something you are not proud of? Have you been tithing? Do you have areas of pain that need healing? Even if we have done some bad things, God wants us to know, "I love you and will never give up on you." This is a time to ask God to make you aware of areas that need mending and attention. Allow God to bring these areas up in your spirit so that they can be addressed. You can fool some people, but you can't fool God! This time leading up to the feast was celebrated in the Bible by a series of shofar or trumpet blasts, blown daily, that build up to a final blowing of blasts at the height of the celebration, the Feast of Trumpets. The blowing of the shofar, or ancient trumpet, was a warning that Rosh Hashanah was coming. We are to be righteous before God. The word righteousness in Hebrew is tsedkah, meaning "charity." Love is translated charity. We are saved because of God's love or charity extended to us. If we are the righteousness of God, his act of charity by grace was extended to mankind. During this time, we should be finding ways to extend charity or help others, showing acts of kindness.

At Rosh Hashanah/The Feast of Trumpets we begin an additional ten day period of repentance. It is a time when He wipes away the last year, and we start clean. But it is imperative that we have ask Jesus Christ into our heart, so that we are grafted into His covenant promises. Believers are to go to the person we have wronged and make amends. If it is not possible to talk with that person, write a letter—God knows your heart and He knows if you have truly forgiven. It is time to make things right. After ten days of making amends, we come to The Day of Atonement. So let's retract back. Thirty days plus ten more make forty days. These forty days are symbolic of when Moses went up the mountain for forty days and God gave him the ten commandments and he came down to find the people were worshiping a golden calf.

He was so upset that he broke the stones that were engraved with the commandments. He then went back up for another forty days to plead with God for forgiveness on behalf of the people. The season of Teshuvah (meaning return or referring to repentance) is linked to these forty days when Moses interceded for the sin of Israel. The Feast of Trumpets starts the ten day period when it is believed that the gate of heaven is uniquely open for petitions and intercession. This period climaxes on the Day of Atonement when offerings were given and there was a time of true repentance before God, and He heard their cry. So the main thing to remember at Rosh Hashanah, or The Feast of Trumpets, is to get yourself ready, repent, offer forgiveness, and prepare your heart. Come clean before a holy God!

God says in Revelation 3:15-16:

(Reader 1) "I know your works, that you are neither cold nor hot. I could wish you were cold or hot. So then, because you are lukewarm, and neither cold nor hot, will I vomit you out of My mouth. (NKJV)

Rosh Hashanah is another name for the Feast of Trumpets. Rosh Hashanah also means "the opening of the gate." When we celebrate a New Year we often reflect and evaluate ourselves and make resolutions for the coming year, right? We also evaluate ourselves on Rosh Hashanah by reflecting back and asking ourselves, "have we been tithing, "or "have we been treating others like we would want to be treated?" "Am I following God's commands to love my neighbor as myself" and "is there anyone I need to forgive?" Am I following God's commandments?" God is opening the gate with all the blessings of heaven. This is a time for true repentance and coming clean before God and starting anew so that He can bless our next twelve months.

Deuteronomy 8:5 says:

(Reader 2) ...as a man chasteneth his son, so the LORD thy God chasteneth thee. (KJV)

Even though God has to reprimand us at times, he still loves us. God has to chasten us so that we can start the New Year with forgiveness and a clean heart. He is blowing the trumpet to remind us that we are starting a new year—let's start with a clean slate. He tells us behold, old things are passed away; all things are becoming new.

This is a very, very special time! It is believed that the destiny of all mankind is recorded by God during this time. He is looking at mankind's heart and true intentions. It is also believed that it is a time that God's book of *blessing* (not to be confused with the book of life, although in a minute we will see that it is likened to the book of life) is opened and we examine our hearts and lives and ask God to write our name in the book of blessing to seal us for a good year.

Rosh Hashanah reminds us of the parable of the ten virgins. The women were virgins because they had received Christ Jesus as their Messiah, and their sins were forgiven and they were washed clean. But the parable tells us that five were foolish and had no oil in their lamps, therefore they were not being lights in the world.

(Reader 3)** And at midnight a cry was heard: "Behold the bridegroom is coming; go out to meet him!" Then all those virgins arose and trimmed their lamps. And the foolish said to the wise, "Give us some of your oil, for our lamps are going out." But the wise answered, saying, "No, lest there should not be enough for us and you; but go rather to those that sell, and buy for yourselves." And while they went to buy, the bridegroom came, and those who were ready went in with him to the wedding; and the door was shut. Afterward the other virgins came also saying, "Lord, Lord, open to us!" But he answered and said, "Assuredly, I say to you, I do not know you." Matthew 25:6-12 (NKJV)

Again this is a warning to be ready, for we know not when Jesus Christ is coming. How many will be left behind?

*Rosh Hashanah/ Feast of Trumpets is the birthday of the creation of Adam and Eve, the *first* man and woman. It emphasizes the close relationship between God and humanity. Remember that there are only ten days between Rosh Hashanah and the Day of Atonement. The Day of Atonement was believed to be the day when Adam sinned and God atoned with the first blood sacrifice of an animal and covered Adam and Eve with the skins of that animal, which by the way most rabbis believe were rams.

So Rosh Hashanah is not only the birthday of creation (when Adam and Eve were created) but also the first anniversary of creation, because Adam and Eve were united together; becoming the *first* family unit. They were the *first* wedding or union, on the earth. God caused Adam to fall asleep; and he removed a rib from his side. From Adam's rib, came Eve. This act resulted in the shedding of blood. Jesus Christ went to the cross and was wounded in the side, thus shedding His blood. The Bible says we are bone of his bone and flesh of his flesh and therefore called the bride of Christ. Revelation 19: 7-9 says:

(Reader 4)***Let us be glad and rejoice, and give honor to him for the marriage of the Lamb is come, and his wife hath made herself ready. And to her was granted that she should be arrayed in fine linen, clean and white for the fine linen is the righteousness of saints. And he saith unto me, Write blessed are they which are called unto the marriage supper of the Lamb. And he saith unto me. These are the true sayings of God. (NKJV)

As the bride of Christ, we need to keep ourselves clean and ready for his return.

I want you to listen to how the High Holy Days (Feast of Trumpets, Day of Atonement, and Feast of Tabernacles) are likened to a marriage.

Jewish traditions teach that a Jewish male wanting to find a bride would come into a village and purchase or pay a price for the bride. (Jesus paid a price on Calvary by shedding his blood) By law the couple was married but considered to be in an engagement phase. They were committed to each other, but living totally separated from each other. The man would leave for at least two years. (Jesus has been gone for two thousand years) He would go to his father's house to prepare a place for him and his wife to live. When ready, his father would say, "Go and get your bride." (Picture of the rapture) When the bridegroom returned, he would send a servant to see if his bride had remained virtuous and had kept her lamp filled with oil. (Oil was likened to the Spirit of God) The virgin, keeping herself ready and having her lamp filled, was a sign that she was watching and waiting for his return. The bridegroom would shout and say at midnight, "the bridegroom cometh." (Likened to Jesus Christ return) The bridegroom would then blow the shofar—signaling his return. Then the bridegroom would take his bride away for seven days to the bridal chamber. (Likened to the seven years-during tribulation) Then they would return and have a party. (Likened to the Feast of Tabernacles) Until Jesus Christ returns for us, we need to be alert, and ready for his return. The father is saying," Get ready, get ready, get ready!

*It is the *only* holiday that is kept for two days. It is also the *only* feast celebrated during the new moon. Scripture says the sky will be dark… referring to a new moon. The other feast is celebrated during the middle of the month, when the moon is full.

Therefore, let's remember the feast of Trumpets is about God *always doing a new thing* as this feast begins with a new moon.

Psalms 40:3says He put a *new song* in my mouth. Isaiah 43:19 says: Behold, I will do a *new thing*; now it shall spring forth: shall ye not know it? I will even make a way in the wilderness, and rivers in the desert. In the beginning of Matthew he makes a *new covenant*, Mark 16:17 says: And these signs shall follow them that believe. In my name shall they cast out devils; they shall speak with *new tongues*. John 2: 7 says: he makes *new wine*. Revelation 21: 5 says: He who was seated on the throne said, "Behold, I make *all things new*. And he said unto me. Write: for these words are true and faithful.

God is all about doing something new and fresh! He said he would trade beauty for ashes. He would turn our morning into laughter. God wants to recreate and mold us and make our bad choices and disaster into a unique and beautiful new piece of art.

It is during the holiest time of the year, that God *looks for us* and confronts us, hoping that we will turn from sin. There are stories in the Bible of men such as Adam, Jonah and Cain, that sinned against God and tried to run or hide. But God confronted them and forced them to own up. But God so lovingly forgave and restored the mess they had made. We live in a world that no one wants to own up to what they have done. We always want to blame someone else for our own mistakes. God just wants honesty and *true repentance*. The Bible says He doesn't condemn, he convicts, to draw you back to him. Satan condemns.

*Rosh Hashanah means Head of the Year. Rosh Hashanah is the *physical* or civil new year, when we were born on the earth. Kind of like our physical birthdays and the day we accepted Jesus Christ as Lord and Savior and were reborn. That's why the sounding of the shofar reminds us to get right! It is not only a change of heart but also a change in action. Psalm 34: 14 says:

(Reader 5)** Turn from evil and do good; seek peace and pursue it.(NIV)

It is a time to check ourselves critically and honestly, with real intentions of changing. Ask God to show us areas we need to repent of and change.

*The central observance of Rosh Hashanah is the sounding of the shofar. The sounding of the shofar is the only commandment specified for His holiday. The sounding of the shofar is a call to mend our ways and to search our hearts before the awesome Day of Judgment. We need to confront our thoughts, our ways, and intensions just as God confronted Adam when he asks, "Where are you?" The Torah or Old Testament calls it the Day of the Awakening Blast from the shofar. There were other reasons for blowing the shofar. The shofar was blown to announce a new king. When Jesus returns in the rapture, the Bible says the trumpet will sound, announcing a king and he will return with a shout. Days prior to the feast of Rosh Hashanah, rabbis blow the shofar. This is a constant reminder for the people" to get ready, get ready, and get ready."

When Jesus returns, he will come as a King to set up the New Jerusalem. Second, it was used to call the army of the Lord to battle. In the story of David and Bathsheba, King David should have gone to battle, with his men. Instead he stayed home, and fell into sin. If we are going to be ready for the rapture, we too need to get in the fight and be ready at all times. Thirdly, the blowing of the shofar is a call to worship. Paul said in Isaiah,

(Reader 6) "Wake up! Hear the sound of the trumpet. Let it awaken you out of your sleep, because if you are asleep, you are not redeeming the time. The King is coming; the Bridegroom is coming; wake up, because when He comes and finds you asleep, and you say, "Lord, don't forget me," it will be too late."

During the Feast of Rosh Hashanah, the shofar or ram's horn is sounded one hundred times on each of the two days. Think about that. If that were being done in today's time, could you imagine hearing the sound of the shofar being blasted over the radio waves or through our phones and broadcast in the streets, one hundred times over the course of the day for two days. It would be hard for anyone to say that they never heard the blast.

Have you taken the time to check your life and to repent and forgive? Do you need to change bad habits? God is not willing that anyone should perish or be left behind. That's why he sounds the shofar over and over, to make people ready!

Psalm 89:15 says:

" Blessed is the people that know the joyful sound: they shall walk, O Lord, in the light of thy countenance." (KJV)

Exodus 19:16:

"And it came to pass on the third day in the morning, that there were thunders and lightening, and a thick cloud upon the mount, and the voice of the trumpet exceeding loud; so that all the people that was in the camp trembled." (KJV)

Exodus 19:19 says:

"And when the voice of the trumpet sounded long, and waxed louder and louder, Moses spake, and God answered him by a voice." (KJV)

God displayed great power when he gave Moses the Ten Commandments. The shofar reminds us to recommit ourselves to God and to live according to his commandments.

The sounding of the shofar is also a symbol of the binding of Isaac. In Genesis 22, we find the story of Abraham and Isaac. Abraham was willing to sacrifice his only son. The *ram, who's horn* was caught in the thicket, was sacrificed in Isaac's place. The ram's horn is a symbol of Abraham's trust in God, even when he was facing the death of his son. This reminds us that we should totally and fully trust God with our lives as well.

*Finally, the most important reason for Rosh Hashanah is that it is a rehearsal of the rapture of the church. Jewish people believe that Jesus will come during the Feast of Trumpets. They are still looking for Messiah. Believers of Christ Jesus also know he is coming… but coming to rapture the church.

1Thessalonians 4:16 says:

"because the Lord Himself will descend from heaven with a shout, with a voice of an archangel, and with a trump of God: and the dead in Christ shall rise first; Then we, which are alive and remain shall be caught up together with them into the clouds, to meet the Lord in the air: and so shall we ever be with the Lord. (KJV)

Matthew 24:30 says:

"At that time the sign of the Son of Man will be appear in the sky, and all the nations of the earth will morn. They will see the Son of Man coming on the clouds of the sky, with power and great glory." (NIV)

And Acts 1:11 says:

Which also said, Ye men of Galilee, why stand ye gazing up into heaven? this same Jesus, which is taken up from you into heaven, shall so come in like manner as ye have seen him go into heaven. (KJV)

*So the sounding of the shofar announces the arrival of the King of Kings. The Bible tells us that no one knows the day or time Jesus will return, but He gives us so many signs. He is not trying to trick us. He is a God of patterns and rhythms. It is not his will that any should parish—He is sounding the alarm! Get ready for He is coming soon! No one wants to be left behind!

*At this time the servers will prepare to bring the food to the tables.

*Let's pray over the food*

We are going to take a few minutes to sample and taste the food that our Jewish friends might be enjoying tonight. I am going to tell you why they may be having these dishes during this celebration.

Refer to Footnote[14]

As you see there are bowls of honey in front of you. We will be dipping apples in the honey. Our Jewish family eat apple with honey to symbolize our desire for a sweet year. As believers in Jesus Christ, we believe him for blessing, abundance and hope for a good, prosperous sweet year ahead. (*Partake of the food*)

Classic honey cake is also a dish made with honey that may appear on some tables. Recipes can be found on the internet. Again representing the

---

14  * Give servers a few minutes to get the food ready to bring out (should already be ready to serve)

sweetness of God and how he is so good and merciful to forgive us of sin, wipe the slate clean and begin new and fresh. (*Partake of the food*)

Challah bread baked in a circle is being served as a wish or hope that the coming year will roll around smoothly without unhappiness or sorrow, and that we will have a blessed year. The bread is also dipped in honey before eating. (*Partake of the food*)

Pomegranate is eaten symbolizing our wish to have a year *full* of good deeds; as a pomegranate is filled with many, many luscious seeds. (*Partake of the food*)

Many eat carrot dishes because in Yiddish the word for carrots means to multiply. It is our hope that God will bless us richly and will greatly multiply an abundance of blessings, and open the windows of heaven over us. Tonight we will be served_____ made from carrots. (*Partake of the food*)

Sweet potato dishes are seen on many tables to represent our desire for a sweet year. Tonight we will be served_____ (*Partake of the Food*)

On many Jewish tables, the head of a fish may be displayed or fish served in the meal…which symbolizes our desire to be the head and not the tail. We declare tonight that we will be the lender and not the borrower, above and not beneath and in a leading position. We are blessed of God!! Therefore, tonight we are being served _____. (*Partake of the food*)

Let's take a few minutes to enjoy the food and company of the friends around you. Then we will finalize our celebration. (*Play Jewish festive music*)

I hope everyone enjoyed the food. We said earlier that some feel the Messiah will come during the Feast of Trumpets, which is very possible, since our God is a God of appointments and He requires the shofar to be blown at this feast. But no one knows the day or time; therefore it is best to be prepared at all times. All of God's feasts are a rehearsal in preparation for the coming of the Lord.

In celebrating God's feast throughout the entire year, we have seen his death, burial and resurrection in the first three Spring Feast—Passover,

Unleavened Bread, and First Fruits. We have seen the giving of his law and the birth of the church during the Feast of Weeks or Pentecost. Now we are making preparation for Messiah's return in these last three celebrations known as the High Holy Days.

Remember that it is during the High Holy Days that we give our final first fruit offering. God says to bring an offering to Him three times a year. (During the Feast of Passover, Feast of Pentecost, and the Feast of Tabernacles) This is a seed offering sown with great expectation that God will give us an exceptionally awesome year to come. Your offering can be given anytime between now and the time of the Feast of Tabernacles. I feel when we start preparing our offering ahead of time, it proves we are earnestly preparing our hearts and are serious about his required offerings, and are looking for a strong move of God—not just throwing something together at the last minute.

In Haggai 2: 19 the prophet says:

> "Is the seed yet in the barn? yea, as yet the vine, and the fig tree, and the pomegranate, and the olive tree, hath *not brought* forth: from *this day* I will bless you." (NIV)

God is telling his people, don't wait! (Don't wait until the vines, the fig trees, pomegranate and olive trees have yielded their fruit-don't wait until you feel you have enough left over to give an offering. God said from *this day* I will bless you. If you never plant the seed …you may never see the harvest God has reserved for you. Don't delay! You can't expect a harvest without planting a seed. We too should look forward to this time, and welcome it with excitement and anticipation looking forward to what God is going to do in the coming year! Remember our tithes are the one tenth of our earnings that we give to God, but our offerings are the three times a year we come before the Lord and we don't come empty handed. (At the feast of God)

(Reader 7) Three times in a year shall all thy males shall appear before the Lord thy God in the place which he shall choose; in the feast of unleavened bread, and in the feast of weeks, and in the feast of tabernacles: and they shall not appear before the Lord empty: Every man shall give as he is able, according to the blessing of the Lord thy God which he hath given thee. (KJV)

*So we should already be thinking about our offerings*

Let me say, ten days from now is the Day of Atonement. There is no feast on this special day. We are required to fast for twenty four hours. This is the holiest day on God's calendar, which is___date_____ this year. Please, please, please don't take this day lightly. There will be a special service for the Day of Atonement. Jesus Christ gave his life as atonement for our sin. Don't miss it!

And four days after that, will be the Feast of Tabernacles, a time of great joy and celebration! So a lot is happening in the next few weeks. I know it may seem like a lot at one time but these are God's appointed times that only come once a year. You only have one chance this year to receive these blessings as God's window of opportunity is passing by you. Please don't miss your appointment with God. He is waiting!

But right now we want to get reverent before the Lord and spend some time examining our hearts. Ask God to cleanse us from all unrighteousness. Ask God to bring up in our memories any sin for which we need to ask forgiveness. Let's be real before God our creator. He knows our weaknesses. He wants to take away our rebellious spirit, and prideful nature. *He wants to do a new thing in our lives.*

Now you can simply bow your head right where you are or you can find a quiet place by yourself to meet with God. But let's meet with our creator at his appointed time.

Keeping a spirit of reverence, let's find a place to pray. As we move to our places, we are going to take a small amount of bread or crumbs and throw them into the _____ (pool of water/bowl of fish). *You will find the crumbs at the body of water.* This is to symbolize that we are casting away our sins or the "old man". This reminded God's people while visiting a body of water like a river or pond with fish in it; that fish are dependent on water and we are dependent on God. A fish's eye's never close; and our God's watchful eyes never cease or close. We are leaving our old ways behind us, and starting a new year with a clean slate. God will cast our sin into the sea of forgetfulness, never to be remembered again!

As you leave, tell someone, "May you be inscribed in the Book of Life."

(Play soft reverent music, Jewish if possible, while people are praying. Keep talking very low and down to a minimum (As to respect others that are praying)

# Day of Atonement/Yom Kippur Preparation List

### Preparation for Service

THIS SERVICE WORKS BEST WHEN held in the sanctuary of a church.

1. Have a table or place set up to accommodate a **menorah or two candles**. (With a **lighter**)

2. **Choose an honorable woman** before the service starts to light the candles. (At the appropriate time) Instruct the woman that lighting the candles signifies ushering in the presence of God. She will waive her hands over the candles three times and place her hands over her eyes and say a silent prayer. Waiving her hands three times over the candles represents bringing in God's light, health, and prosperity. If using a menorah, the menorah represents the presence of God.

3. A **shofar** can be placed on the table as well, to be blown at the beginning and at the end of the service. (A cd with the sounding of the shofar can be used if no one has or can play the shofar)

4. Have **handouts**[15] ready to be passed out to your guests:

5. Readings

6. Have a **basket** prepared for the offerings

---

15  Handout with blessing/ A Few Areas of Prayer

# Day of Atonement/Yom Kippur: At One With God

**(Script for Leader)**

Would everyone stand as we welcome the presence of God?

***Have an honorable woman light the candles***

Everyone repeat out loud:

Hear O Israel, the Lord is our God, the Lord is one.

*Blow the shofar*

Leviticus 23: 26-28 says:

> The Lord spake unto Moses, saying, Also on the tenth day of this seventh month there shall be a day of atonement: it shall be a holy convocation unto you; and ye shall afflict your souls, (fast) and offer an offering made by fire unto the Lord. And ye shall do no work in that same day; for it is a day of atonement, to make an atonement for you before the Lord your God." (KJV)

**Let's pray**

"Happy New Year" Most new year's start with the blowing of party horns and flying confetti. God's New Year starts with the blowing of a horn as well, the shofar. This is the "new year" on God's calendar. He is ready to wipe our slate clean so that we can begin the year with a fresh, new beginning. We began the year with the Feast of Trumpets, alerting us to get ready; check your hearts, find forgiveness, and clear your conscience. Tonight we are celebrating the Day of Atonement; when He blots out and takes away our sin and completely wipes away every iniquity and curse from our life.

Today is God's holy Day Of Atonement.

How many of you know that most of the miracles Jesus performed were in Jerusalem, on the way to Jerusalem or around the Sea of Galilee? Have you ever thought about why that was? Jesus was a practicing Jew, and would have been participating in the feast. He went to Jerusalem for the feast as would the rest of the Jewish people. The Bible says the feast was to be for all time and to *never* end…continuing them from generation to generation. It was during the time of the feast, particularly during the High Holy Days, (which is right now) that the priest would stand in a high place in the city and blow the shofar, over and over and over. This was to alert the people, it's time, get ready, get ready! It reminded them to prepare their hearts and get their lives in order. If they wanted a fresh start and God's blessing to be on their lives for the next twelve months, they had to get their hearts right before God!

You see they understood that this was the "one time a year" God had set aside and ordained as a holy convocation to blot out their sin and bless his people. As God is the same yesterday, today, and forever there is a window of blessing passing over us right now that only comes one time a year. Its true God is always blessing us throughout the year; but these are specific times he himself has set up to give us a clean, fresh start. He knows we are human and are going to mess up. Most of us, right now, can recall times this past year that we have botched things up. But God is saying; let me wipe the slate clean. He wants to give his children every good thing, overflowing abundance, prosperity, and joy. He wants to break off strongholds that we are carrying and have brought into our lives because of sin. He wants to free us from this year's bondage and baggage and for some people, a life time of baggage; God wants his children free, not just from the sin but the iniquities as well—*totally free!* We should be constantly purging our lives of the junk and clutter.

Just as we have a spring cleaning—we should at least have a yearly purging. Take notice of what you have allowed to come into your body and life. Remember we are the temple of God. Can God freely live and move in you? Are you a fully yielded vessel that He can use? Or are there areas of bitterness, resentment, anger and unforgiveness that is taking up valuable space distracting you from giving God your total attention? This is why He is sounding the alarm!

Remember the fall feast began with a thirty day time period leading up to the Feast of Trumpets/Rosh Hashanah nudging us to ask God to make us aware of areas in our life that need to be addressed or need forgiveness.

We then had The Feast of Trumpets reminding us to get ready and get our lives in order. The next ten days known as the Days of Awe, bid us to make amends with anyone we have ought with or need forgiveness. Sincerely ask God to search your heart; repent, repent, repent. Clean up your life! Get your heart clean and pure before a holy God, because, tonight brings us to The Day of Atonement! This day is the most holy day on God's calendar. That word atonement, broken up is "at one." God wants *intimacy* with you. He wants to be "one" with you.

You see, if you truly love God—you die to man's carnal, selfish, lustful ways and allow him to have control of your life, so he can release his love out through you. But God is *holy* and cannot inhabit a dirty vessel. He is not going to live in something Defiled with sin, pride, rebellion, selfishness, and corruption. He cannot tolerate a controlling spirit, that is full of themselves. When we have these things present in our lives we really limit how much God can use us. (And we wonder why He doesn't use us more.)

Let's start in the Old Testament; on the Day of Atonement, the High Priest would bring a bull and two goats to be sacrificed. The Priest would wash his whole body and put on a clean robe. The priest himself had to be holy before God, just as it is imperative today for the preacher, Rabbi, teacher, or anyone that is leading or teaching people to have their lives pure and holy before God. God demands holiness! Now the priest would kill a bull first, for the sins of himself and his family. Two goats were brought before an altar. The first goat was slaughtered and his blood was poured into a bowl for the sin of the people. The priest would put his thumb and forefinger in the blood and would sprinkle the Mercy Seat seven times (representing the seven places Jesus shed his blood to break every curse off of our lives) and would then place his hand on the head of the second goat. The second goat became the scape goat. This is where the term" scape goat" originated.

He laid hands on the goats and symbolically transferred the sin of the people onto the scape goat. So the first goat was the sacrifice, the one that provided atonement. The second was the scape goat. The scape goat carried the curse of the sin away. The scape goat was then led into the wilderness to die, removing the sin from the people.

Rabbinical teachers say that during the ceremony, a crimson sash was attached to the door of the temple and to the horn of the scape goat. When the goat died, the crimson sash would turn white. This let the people know that their sins had been forgiven and the curse was broken. Forty years before the destruction of the temple, the sash stopped turning white. This is because forty years before the destruction of the Temple, something magnificent happened, Jesus Christ died on a cross. The Bible says: though your sins are as scarlet, they are white as snow. Jesus Christ was crucified and slaughtered at Calvary, mutilated, beaten and whipped for our sins. God our pure and holy High Priest, allowed His son Jesus Christ, to redeem us by becoming the scape goat for our sin.

Jesus Christ died on a cross and carried our sins away. So no longer do we need to sacrifice rams and bulls and goats. Jesus Christ became the ultimate sacrifice for the sins of the world by the shedding of his blood. His blood is now the atonement for our sins and for breaking off the curses on our life as a result of our sins! (Two separate things) He has provided double freedom. Simply put, free from the sin itself and on top of that, free from the curse or moral liability of our sin—the iniquity, (because of the way he died—on a cross.) The Bible says cursed is the man who dies on a tree. So Jesus Christ died on a cross for the sin *and* the iniquity of our sin as well! God's plan is complete and perfect. God wants his people not only free, but *free indeed!* Let me say as well, animal sacrifices under the Mosaic Covenanent only "covered" the sin, but the atonement of Yeshua "removed" sin.

The shedding of blood has always been a requirement for the forgiveness of sin. Yeshua, through his death on a tree, paid the ultimate price for our sins to be removed once and for all—not just blotted over. During that time, intentional sins like adultery, could not be blotted out by the sacrifice of an animal—the guilty person themselves paid the price with their lives. Praise God, when Jesus Christ gave his life, all sin was covered.

The Day of Atonement is also known as Yom Kippur. In the Hebrew, Yom Kippur is Yom Kippur Kiffer, which is where we get the word kiffer, which means in Hebrew, to seal. Remember, Noah was told by God to build the ark and to use a pitch called in Hebrew, "Kiffer." He used this to seal the grooves and cracks of the ark to keep it from leaking. It was used as a sealant for protection. Since kiffer means to seal and atonement means "to cover," we see why this word is used for the Day of Atonement.

God wants to not only blot out and cover our sins, but remove them completely and seal us for a good year. Noah used a pitch called kiffer to seal the ark—which was a type of covering or atonement. It kept the ark sealed and dry and safe from the elements and water. Jesus Christ blood was a covering or atonement that sealed us and completely covered us and separated us from our sin. Satan cannot penetrate or pass through the blood covering. When our sins are washed and covered in the blood; we are forgiven of the sin and set free from the iniquity (or tendency to be pulled back to the sin) when we understand that our sin was erased when Jesus Christ shed his life's blood but the iniquity was removed as well by the way in which he died—on a tree. Up until the destruction of the second temple in Jerusalem in 70 A.D. people were offering animal sacrifices for atonement from sin. But after the temple was destroyed, they had no place to sacrifice. Messiah Yeshua became the ultimate sacrifice by dying on a cross and giving his blood. Now our sins are not just blotted over but removed forever. Yearly sacrificing of animals was no longer needed. The price was paid. *There is power in the blood!*

Atonement is also associated with repentance. Re—means to return and pent—means at the highest point. God wants us to turn from our sin, or evil ways, and go back to our highest point. The highest point would be to go back to the Garden of Eden, before sin was present. Adam and Eve were taken out of the garden because of their prideful nature and lack of repentance. They both blamed someone else instead of being humble and taking full responsibility for their own actions. God wants intimate and close communion with us. If we're not willing to repent and lose the pride and come clean before a holy God we cannot have that communion with Him—because *He is holy* and righteous, and without sin.

In the Old Testament there was a sin offering and a guilt offering. The *sin* offering represented sin against almighty God and the *guilt* offering represented sin against another person. The guilt offering had to be offered first. So if you had offended someone or if someone had wronged you, you had to receive forgiveness from them first before giving an offering to God, because God would not receive your offering if you had ought with your brother. That had to be addressed first. God would not heal you and bless you until you got your relationships with others in order. (I wander if that might be why more people are not healed today? Just saying) Once you had forgiven, God would forgive you. Let's think and ponder for a moment. If I said the name of someone and the first thing that popped into your head was not feelings of love, joy, and peace, but anger, resentment and frustration, then there is a good chance you need to resolve an issue with that person. Feelings of anger and hatred are not God qualities.

The ten days leading up to Yom Kippur or the Day of Atonement were known as the Ten Days of Repentance or the Days of Awe. During this time we are encouraged to seek out anyone we have offended and ask for forgiveness so we can start the New Year with a clean slate. This is very important to God and he knows your heart. He knows if you are too prideful to resolve your issues. It isn't easy to humble yourself and confront that person to resolve an issue—but it's imperative because God knows the condition of your heart and how it can cause a perpetual wound. The wounds and hurt becomes a foot hold that Satan uses to bring disease, depression and demonic oppressions on us. *We* give him legal right to do so by not forgiving and therefore leaving the door open to Satan. He is intently watching our lives and looking for any opportunity. Remember, God writes the names in the book of blessing. He sees your heart and intent. If you still have unresolved issues tonight—repent before God and resolve them as soon as possible. There is a window of opportunity passing by. He does not want you to miss out. He is giving you every opportunity. Unforgiveness results in bondage *for you not the other person.*

Speaking of forgiveness, The Day of Atonement commemorates the day God forgave the Jewish people for the sin of worshipping the golden calf. After receiving the Ten Commandments and hearing God say at Mt. Sinai, "You should have no other gods before me, and you shall not make for yourselves any graven image," the Jews committed this sin, by making and worshipping a golden calf. Moses went back up the mountain for forty more days pleading to God on their behalf for their forgiveness. This day was celebrated annually from then on as "The Day of Atonement." Hence, the thirty days (Month of Elul) plus the ten Days of Awe, total forty days. God forgave them once again. The Day of Atonement is considered the most solemn day of the whole year and the most holy day on God's calendar. God is still forgiving our sin today and sealing us for a good year.

Another important area of Atonement was in fasting and prayer. Leviticus 23: 27 describe it as "afflicting your souls" which means abstaining from food or drink, and from any sexual activity, which is in essence denying the flesh.

Matthew 6: 16-18 says:

**Reader #1 ****Moreover when ye fast, be not, as the hypocrites, of a sad countenance: for they disfigure their faces, that they may appear unto men to fast. Verily I say unto you, They have their reward. But thou, when thou fastest, anoint thine head, and wash thy face; That thou appear not unto men to fast, but unto thy Father which is in secret: and thy Father, which seeth in secret, shall reward thee openly. (JKV)***

We are to abstain from food and drink and sexual activity for twenty four hours on the Day of Atonement. We have a body and a soul. Our bodies seldom fail to let us know when we are hungry or thirsty or cold. Our body constantly lets us know what it needs. Our souls also speak out but are a little harder to hear. Just as we don't hear the refrigerator running during the day because of noise around us, it is still on. But we hear it running when the house is quiet. It is the same for our souls, when we deny our bodies, we can hear clearly what our souls are saying. God wants us to have a good balance between the two." Just as our bodies need the necessities of life, food and water—our souls also need attention, such as a relationship with God, emotional interaction, etc.

Therefore, when we commit to a day of afflicting our souls or fasting, we are telling our bodies we are not listening to its needs today; we are listening to what our souls are saying. We are also instructed not to work on the Day of Atonement. Again, we are cutting off all distractions so that we can check ourselves and get our lives in order. (I realize we do not live in Israel and most of us are required to work to keep our jobs—we are living in an imperfect world where we are forced to make the best decision we can—I think God knows our heart, intentions and our desire to please him. Try to follow God's commands as closely as you can. As we live in this imperfect world, we are going to be faced with decisions where we have to personally seek God for direction.

It's also a time to check ourselves in areas that may be affecting others around you. "Is what I am wearing affecting others in a negative way?" "Is what I am doing or saying causing others to sin as well?" "Am I doing this particular good deed but for the wrong reasons. The main thing is for the next twenty four hours; commit ourselves to prayer and repentance.

Clean the junk out of our lives. Make ourselves a living sacrifice, holy and acceptable before God.

Is fasting important to God? The Bible says, "When you fast," not if you want to fast. People fasted in Bible. We are commanded to fast. Jesus himself fasted. He had been fasting for forty days when he was tempted by Satan. The national of Israel fasted for three days and nights. The disciples fasted. Paul and Daniel fasted. Moses, Joshua, and Elijah fasted for forty days. I believe fasting turns the face of God. It shows him we are serious and desperate for him. I believe everyone can fast something. Some do a partial fast, some fast all food and only drink water or juice, some do a Daniel fast, but everyone can deny themselves something for God.

Abraham Lincoln instituted a day of prayer and fasting for our nation; many of our leaders believed in prayer and fasting. But because of sin, we have brought curses onto our land and our country is rotting and decaying. Instead of repenting, we have vowed to build a stronger and mightier country, as was the same curse on Israel. The Bible teaches," *if my people who are called by my name* will humble themselves and pray and seek my face and turn from their wicked ways *then* I will hear from heaven and *I will* heal their land." Let's repeat this prayer together and renounce the curse that we have brought on our country.

> "Our Father God and creator of the universe,—we, your people— who are called by your name,—have sinned against you.— We humble ourselves—and repent for our wicked ways.—We repent and renounce—any vows we made against you.—We are totally dependent on you—and look to you for restoration—We repent for hatred—against your chosen people, the Jews.—We plead the blood of Calvary—over the sin of our nation—as we pray and seek your face.—You said that then,—you would hear from heaven—and you would heal our land.—Lord, hear the sincere prayers of your people.—Hear our repentance—and heal our nation.—Amen

We need prayer and fasting more than ever for our nation.

What are the benefits from fasting? It gives us spiritual and supernatural power. Luke 4:14 says they came out of the fast with power. Fasting can bring deliverance from unclean spirits-the Bible says this kind only comes out with prayer and fasting. Fasting can bring deliverance from addictions. It gives us wisdom for making decisions, brings healing for the body and soul. Fasting cleans and purifies the toxins from our bodies so that our bodies work at optimal levels. Fasting is something we believers should be doing regularly. We are commanded to fast!

Listen to the words of Joel 2:12-14 (NIV) in Hebrew it reads:

Reader #2 *** "Even now," declares the Lord, "return to me with all your heart, with fasting and weeping and morning." Rend your heart and not your garments, Return to the Lord your God, for he is gracious and compassionate, slow to anger and abounding in love,and he relents from sending calamity. Who knows? He may turn and have pity and leave behind a blessing—grain offerings and drink offerings for the Lord your God.

Reader #3 ***Blow the trumpet in Zion. Declare a holy fast, call a sacred assembly. Gather the people, consecrate the assembly; bring together the elders, gather the children, those nursing at the breast. Let the bridegroom leave his room and the bride her chamber. Let the priests, the minister before the LORD, weep between the temple porch and the alter. Let them say, "Spare your people, O LORD, Do not make your inheritance an object of scorn, a byword among the nations. Why should they say among the peoples, Where is their God?" Then the LORD will be jealous for his land and take pity on his people. The LORD will reply to them: I am sending you grain, new wine and oil, enough to satisfy you fully: never again will I make you an object of scorn to the nations. I will drive the northern army far from you, pushing it into a parched and barren land, with its front columns going into the eastern sea and those in the rear into the western sea. And its stench will go up; its smell will rise." Surely he has done great things. Be not afraid, O land; be glad and rejoice. Surely the LORD has done great things. Be not afraid, O wild animals, for the open pastures are becoming green. The trees are bearing their fruit; the fig tree and the vine yield their riches. Be glad, O people of Zion, rejoice in the LORD your God, for he has given you the autumn rains in righteousness. He sends you abundant showers, both autumn and spring rains, as before. The threshing floors will be filled with grain; the vats will overflow with new wine and oil. "I will repay you for the years the locust swarm—my great army that I sent among you. You will have plenty to eat, until you are full, and you will praise the name of the LORD your God, who has worked wonders for you; never again will my people be ashamed. Then you will know that I am in Israel, that I am the LORD your God, and that there is no other; never again will my people be shamed. Joel 2: 15-27 (NIV)

Reader #4 **"And afterward, I will pour out my Spirit on all people. Your sons and daughters will prophesy, your old men will dream dreams, your young men will see visions. Even on my servants, both men and women, I will pour out my Spirit in those days. I will show wonders in the heavens and on the earth, blood and fire and billows of smoke. The sun will be turned to darkness and the moon to blood before the coming of the great and dreadful day of the LORD. Joel 2: 28-31 (NIV)

These verses mention seven supernatural blessings on the Day of Atonement *if* we repent, pray, and fast. He will seal us for the coming year with: A double portion, financial blessing, miracles, restoration, God's presence, family blessing, and deliverance.

God also requires us to bring our final offering for the year. We are taught in scripture to bring our tithes and offerings to God. Remember our tithes are the first ten percent of our earnings that are given regularly. We have been taught that offerings are what we give above and beyond our tithes. But in fact, our offerings are given at feast times, the three times a year we come before the Lord and we don't come empty handed: The Feast of Passover, The Feast of Pentecost, and The Feast of Tabernacles. We are to give our final offering by the time of the last feast—The Feast of Tabernacles. Some bring their final offering early anytime during the High Holy Days. When we bring our final first fruit offering, we are promised a double-portion blessing: The former rain and the later rain in the first month. The former rain deals with the spring rains, preparing the land for the seed. The latter rain deals with the fall outpouring when the land is prepared for harvest. During the first month of God's calendar, which is where we are right now, both rains come together for those who are obedient to bring their offering to God. If obedient with our offerings—he will be faithful to bring a downpour of blessing into our lives!"

At this time, we are going to bring our first fruit offering and place it in the appropriate basket. If you have already given your offering ahead of time but wish for the Pastor (Rabbi) to speak blessing over it, you may write on a piece of paper "first fruit offering given in advance" and place it in the basket—God sees the intent of the heart. If some are not prepared tonight to give their offering, we will again receive an offering at the Feast of Tabernacles, when God seals our blessing. As you become more familiar with the feast and offerings, you will want to start preparing your offerings and putting it aside ahead of time and praying and seeking God for guidance. These offering are not intended to be a last minute thought, although tonight we are just learning about the offerings and becoming familiar with them—You'll begin to plan ahead. God doesn't need your money; He needs your obedience. Remember if a farmer doesn't plant seed he cannot expect a harvest. When it was time for the feast, the people were glad to come to the house of the Lord with their offerings. They were excited for these times of giving because they understood that it was a unique opportunity for great blessing that only came once a year!

\*\*If you are prepared tonight I would ask you to come forward with your offering and place it in the basket\*\*

Father God, as we bring our offerings, we declare it to be no longer tainted by the world's system, but blessed and consecrated to you. We declare that it has passed from this corrupt earthly kingdom into God's kingdom, so that He can multiply it for the work of the Lord and can bring blessing and prosperity and joy and hope and peace to the people of God. Lord, it gives us great joy to bring our offering before you in obedience. It is you, who gives us divine opportunities and wisdom to capture the wealth you have placed on the earth. You said in your word that you are the One who gives us the ability to make money. May the wealth of the wicked be placed in the hands of the righteous? Help us to realize we are blessed to be a blessing to others. Amen.

\*\*At this time the Pastor (*Or Rabbi*) is going to receive our offerings and "set it" on the alter before the Lord of Hosts by laying his hand over the offering and saying a prayer of blessing over it.

\*\*Pastor (*Or Rabbi*) comes forward and says a prayer over the offering\*\*

We want to spend the rest of our time tonight with our creator. We no longer need a mediator or a high priest to go on our behalf before God; we can go boldly before Him ourselves. Let's take our petitions to Him right now. Be sure to get your heart right before Him and make sure there is no un-forgiveness still present. Find a spot and just sit or kneel in His presence and bask in His love. Tell Him how much you love and adore Him. Take some time to just love on Him. Talk to Him about areas in your life that are broken or need fixing.

**Use the handout as a guide to help you pray for different areas in your life. In the course of your day tomorrow, read the Torah readings from the Bible that coincides with the Day of Atonement—as they can be found on the internet.

Refer to Footnote[16]

*If possible, at the end of the service the shofar is sounded signifying the end of the high holy days.*

We are confident that God has sealed us all for a wonderful year: a year of happiness, prosperity, health, joy and peace. May we all leave with His blessing and favor and carry His anointing. Amen

---

16 Play soft reverent music in the background while we seek the Lord

# The Feast of Tabernacles/ Sukkot Preparation List

## Food and Preparation List Needed:

1. Place two tables together making one large table to accommodate twelve people. Paper table cloths are used to conveniently be thrown away after.

2. I like to set up a tent in the middle of the room, with the tables arranged around the **tent** to represent a booth or tabernacle. **Stringing lights** on the tent and candles everywhere on the tables is a good touch since this feast is distinguished from other feast by its lights. (God is the light of the world) I like to use battery candles. Vegetables and crops can also be hanging down from the tent, representing a good harvest. These are just ideas of my own; you might come up with something else or another arrangement of the tables to fit your group.

3. Tables are decorated to resemble a **Thanksgiving theme**. Cornucopias are great to use representing a bountiful harvest. Fall flowers and fruits and vegetables are fun to decorate with as well,

as this is a time of harvest. One can be as elaborate or conservative as you like.

4.  A table is set up at the front for the speaker to stand by. It too is decorated for a bountiful harvest.

5.  **Two candles or a menorah** with a lighter is placed on the table to be lit by a woman. (Chosen prior to starting)

6.  A cup of **wine or juice** is placed on the table of the speaker

7.  **"Four species"** is set on the speaker's table (*description found on line*) or if unable to locate, a picture of the four species is used

8.  One can eat about anything at this feast, but it is particularly common to have **foods that are stuffed.** Think of it as having small cornucopias. (A bountiful harvest) Some ideas are ravioli stuffed with cheese and sauce, stuffed spinach and fruit stuffed with cream filling, stuffed cream puffs and dough nuts stuffed with filling, to mention a few. Many people like chella bread—this could be infused or stuffed with honey. A round loaf of bread hollowed out in the middle and stuffed with a bread dip. An olive oil, herbs and vinegar combination is a great idea. The ideas are endless as to what you might choose to have at your feast.

9.  **Festive Jewish music** is played while people are coming in and during the meal.

10. Keep in mind these are all just suggestions that I put together to make the feast fun, remember able and honorable to OUR GOD while including a hint of Jewish culture as we worship Him together as one new man!

# The Feast of Tabernacles/Sukkot: God Working in and Through Us

**(Script for Leader)**

Let's begin by lighting the candles. (*A woman comes forward to light the candles.*) John 8:12 says: …"I am the light of the world."..(KJV)

During the time of temple worship, at the Feast of Tabernacles, a lightening ceremony took place. Four huge candelabrums, each seventy five feet tall, were lit in what was called the Court of the Women. Now the light from the candelabrums was so great that it lit the entire region. This was to say, one day, Messiah would come; and He would be the light of the world. The one thing that distinguishes this feast tonight, the Feast of Tabernacles, from all of the other feasts, is the *lights*.

Does this feast remind you of any certain holiday that we Americans participate in? Look at the tables. Yes, it's Thanksgiving. It occurs at almost the same time of the year. According to historians, the pilgrims actually had the first Thanksgiving on and possibly directly inspired by Sukkot or the feast of tabernacles. The pilgrims were a very religious people. When they came out of Europe they compared themselves to Israel coming out of Egypt. The pilgrims compared God bringing them across the Atlantic

Ocean to the Israelites passing through the Red Sea; both were headed to a Promise Land, to worship the God of Abraham, Isaac, and Jacob. They wanted to be free from the persecution of England and the Catholic Church, they called themselves Judeo-Christians.

As we look around, we have a booth or tent in the middle of the room. God told his people to build a booth to stay in for seven days. The Feast of Tabernacles is a seven day celebration. They still build tents today and hang fall crops around in the booth or tent to acknowledge God's faithfulness in providing for His people while they were in the dessert.

Before we go any further, let's invite our guest of honor, the presence of God, into this place and invite him to tabernacle with us as we give him all the glory and honor rightfully due him tonight for the many blessings of life and for his goodness. Let's invite him to take permanent residence in our lives and in our hearts, not just tonight but always.

**Let's pray**

Let's review the feast we have honored this year. Our first time together, was honoring three of the spring feast, starting with ridding ourselves of our pride in the Feast of Unleavened Bread. We were delivered from bondage and set free as Jesus Christ became our Passover lamb in the Feast of Passover. We learned in the Feast of First Fruits to bring our best offering three times a year. God gave us a pathway or guideline to follow along with the Holy Spirit giving us fire, anointing, wisdom, and authority to live a life free from bondage as seen in the Feast of Pentecost. Then the fall feast began, with the blowing of the shofar, bearing a reminder to get our lives in order; check our heart, seek forgiveness; for the glorious coming of Messiah is at hand as seen in the Feast of Trumpets. Next we celebrated the holiest day of the year, The Day of Atonement, when blood was shed and our sins were forgiven. No longer do we have to make blood sacrifices of bulls or doves or lambs because Jesus Christ became the ultimate sacrifice, shedding his own blood for the remission of our sin. He became the lamb that takes away the sin of the world. So this brings us to our celebration tonight of the Feast of Tabernacles.

Remember we said the High Holy Days, which are a combination of the fall Feast of Trumpets, Day of Atonement, and the Feast of Tabernacles, were likened to a Jewish wedding. But our feast tonight is the part of the marriage where the bridegroom returns with the bride, and they have a huge party. (The marriage supper of the Lamb) He showers us with gifts or rewards (Bema seat) and it is truly a time of celebration. Sukkot or the Feast of Tabernacles is a picture of the Marriage of the Lamb, the making of the New Covenant, and the establishment of the Kingdom of God on earth. It is a picture of the millennial reign, when Christ reigns on earth for one thousand years and we see the great harvest of souls.

I find it very interesting that to God, his feasts are so important, that in Zechariah 14: 16 it says this:

**Reader#1 And it shall come to pass, that every one that is left of all the nations which came against Jerusalem shall even go up from year to year to worship the King, the Lord of hosts, and to keep the feast of tabernacles. (KJV)**

The scripture is talking about the thousand year reign when Christ will return to the earth with his saints and set up his rule. There will be a thousand years of peace and prosperity. It is during this time, that all the nations (referring in Hebrew to the gentiles or non-Jews) and people *will be required every year*, to worship Christ and take part in the *Feast of Tabernacles*. If the nations still won't obey, there shall be the plaque, wherewith the Lord will smite the heathen.

**** "And it shall be that whoso will not come up of all the families of the earth unto Jerusalem to worship the King, the Lord of hosts, even upon them shall be no rain."

During that time, even the Gentiles (non-Jewish people) will have to keep this feast. The feasts are generally thought to be "Jewish" feast, and that we do not need to keep or remember them. But the Bible calls them God's feast. God *did say* His feast were to be kept from *generation to generation—* never ending!

Jesus Christ kept the feast of tabernacles. We see in John chapter 7, that he devoted an entire chapter, to describe what Jesus said and did during the Feast of Tabernacles in the last year of His ministry. This tells us how important these feasts were to God. When he said the feasts are forever, they are truly never ending.

** Reader #2***"Thou shalt observe the feast of tabernacles seven days, after that thou hast gathered in thy corn and thy wine: And thou shalt rejoice in thy feast, thou, and thy son, and thy daughter....Seven days shalt thou keep a solemn feast unto the Lord thy God in the place which the Lord shall choose: because the Lord thy God shall bless thee in all thine increase, and in all the works of thine hands, therefore thou shalt surely rejoice... and they shall not appear before the Lord empty: Every man shall give as he is able, according to the blessing of the Lord thy God which he hath given thee. (KJV) Deut. 16: 13-17.

This passage describes Sukkot/ Feast of Tabernacles to us.

Just coming out of Yom Yippur also called the Day of Atonement, leaves us with a solemn or reverent respect. Remember the Day of Atonement is the holiest day of the year. It has to be breath taking to be in Israel during the Day of Atonement. Jewish people do not work on this day and they fast from food and drink. The stores and entertainment venues are closed. The streets lie empty of cars and public transportation of any kind. Television and radio are not being broadcast. They spend most of their day studying and in synagogue. They focus only on repentance. It is the most solemn and holy day on the Jewish calendar. They meditate on how God has sustained them and kept them over the years and that He will continue to keep them. On this Day of Atonement, a sacrifice was made by the High Priest for the sins of the world. Since Jesus Christ has become our ultimate sacrifice, by dying on the cross, we no longer need to sacrifice animals. But, during the time of the Feast of Tabernacles we are told to bring a sacrifice or offering and appear before the Lord thy God according to the blessing of the Lord thy God as he is able.

When we hear the word "sacrifice" we automatically think of killing something. Sacrifice is thought of in a negative way. But it means "a gift." We are to bring the very best gift we have to our Father. We are also to give it with a joyful heart. When we give our best sacrifice or offering, God says this:

**Reader #3*** ...Test me in this," says the Lord Almighty," and see if I will not throw open the floodgates of heaven and pour out so much blessing that you will not have room enough for it." Malachi 3: 10 (NIV)

How is God saying to test Him? In the offering talked about in Malachi 3: 4—the first fruits offering is what Israel had abandoned. God is telling them to return to those offerings and *then* they will see the poured out blessing.

We have been taught that our tithes are the one tenth of our wages that we give to God and the offerings are what we give above and beyond that. ..right? But the offerings are actually the three times a year you come before the Lord and you don't come empty handed: at Passover, Pentecost and Tabernacles. God teaches us to give through the parable of sowing and reaping.

As a farmer has to sow a crop to get a harvest, we too have to sow a seed so that God can multiply it back to us. This principal of sowing works in the spiritual and in the natural realm. If we sow joy, we reap joy. If we sow bitterness, we become bitter. And if we are obedient with our offerings, God brings them back to us in abundance.

So right now, if there are any who have not yet brought your offering or sacrifice and would like to do so, we are going to receive them now in the basket and have Pastor set them before the Lord and offer them to God. If you have sent them in already to a ministry but wish to have our Pastor pray over them, write this acknowledgement on a piece of paper and place it in the basket. (Most of you may have already sent in your offering at the Day of Atonement.) Remember, tonight is when God seals the book of blessing. Do we have a clear conscience? The father has been searching our heart and sees our true intentions. Now we joyfully give our final offering to Him.

**Pastor (*Rabbi*) comes forward to pray**

In Israel, the rains normally stop in March. There is usually very little or no rain for almost seven months. They would pray and cry out to God for the early rain that comes in October and November. If it did not rain, there was famine resulting in no spring crops. This is why the feast was so important to them; they needed God to answer prayer and bring the rain. How many of us are in a dry, desert place. Do we need to hear from God or are we desperate for God to move on our behalf? In Israel, there are two annual harvest seasons. In the spring or first season, the grains are harvested. Later on in the fall, comes the main harvest of fruit. The harvest year ended at the beginning of autumn when the Feast of Tabernacles, also called the feast of ingathering, was held. Listen closely, Pentecost gives us a picture of the early harvest, when the Holy Spirit fell and revival came giving a harvest of three thousand souls; and the Feast of Tabernacles gives us a picture of the fall harvest—which is compared to *The Great Harvest of Souls during the millinnium*, when Jesus Christ rules and reigns for a thousand years.

So what exactly is commanded in the Bible regarding the Feast of Tabernacles?

1. Gather the "4 species"—Leviticus 23: 40 a palm tree branch, myrtle branches, the branch of a willow tree, and an etrog

2. Live in a sukkot—Leviticus 23: 42 and

3. Rejoice before the Lord—Deuteronomy 16: 13-14 and Lev. 23: 40

The four species are a palm tree branch, myrtle branches, the willow of a tree and an etrog. They are bound together, except for the etrog. We are told to take these four plants and use them to rejoice before the Lord, by reciting a blessing and waving the species in six directions. (The north, south, east, and west, up and down) This symbolizes the fact that God is everywhere.

The different plants are symbolizing the different parts of the body of Christ or representing different kinds of Jews. The Gentiles can really appreciate this because we are grafted into the family even though we are different.

Since we are living away from Israel, it is sometimes hard to gather the four species; but if we are unable to have them; you will find a picture of them on your plate. Take the picture home and waive it before the Lord and let it be a reminder that God is everywhere. God knows our desire to follow him.

Why does he want us to remember living in a sukkot or a booth? We all are familiar with the deliverance of Israel from Egypt. Israel should have perished and died many times. But God was always faithful and provided a way of safety for His people; he also provided for their needs.

They left with all the wealth and the spoils. God parted the sea for them to safely get to the other side. God provided for their physical needs by sending manna from heaven every day and water from a rock. They experienced no sickness and their shoes never wore out. So that they would not forget the awesome miracles God had performed, He told them to construct "booths" to serve as a reminder of their temporary living conditions and dwellings as they passed through the wilderness. This reminded them that God was *the only one* that healed and delivered them. We too want to remember that God destroys our enemies and provides food and water and takes care of *all* of our needs, doesn't he? It is so easy to quickly forget the blessings of God and how He takes care of us. The people were told to build a small tabernacle yearly to dwell in for seven days. While wandering around in the wilderness for forty years, they built these booths or shelters so that they could easily be taken down. They were constructed so that they could see through the tops of the sukkots—because God was leading them with a cloud by day and a pillar of fire by night. This is our reminder that no matter how blessed we are, we are to keep our eyes on God, because he is our covering and our provider and protection.

We couldn't live without God. The Israelites had to depend on God for supernatural provision. The desert had no food or water and there were no places to buy necessities. For forty years, they depended on Jehovah Jireh, their provider, to meet their needs. Even today, Jews all over the world continue to keep Sukkot by building booths outside their house. These booths should remind us that this world is just our temporary home—one day we are going to leave this place and tabernacle with our Father forever!

Sukkot is also a time of harvest—not just a time to harvest souls, but to harvest financial blessing, to declare salvation for our families, and to declare that all curses be broken off of our lives.

Let's take a moment….as we are joint heirs with Christ/same authority, meaning we have full access to the father's throne, (*Whatsoever you bind/ shall be bound in heaven and whatsoever you loose*) and declare a harvest of prosperity, the soul of lost loved ones to come to Christ and curses to be broken. Over the last month, as we have confessed our sins, reversed the curses on our lives and applied the blood over these areas and God has released the blessing.

Now as an outward symbol, sometime tonight- I want you to go by the designated areas—and just wash your hands over the bowl using the picture of water. After having done these things…we wash our hands signifying baptism—we are washing off the spirit of failure on our life and starting over.

\*\*Pray\*\*

Sukkot is a time of rejoicing and celebrating the birth of our Lord, Jesus Christ. Most of us have grown up celebrating Jesus' birthday on December 25. Jesus Christ's birth has been traced back to Mary conceiving Jesus during Hunnakah or around Christmas time. Nine months later would have put his birth during Sukkot, or the festival of lights. Sukkot in Hebrew means stable. It is also interesting that it says Jesus was wrapped in swaddling clothes. Swaddling clothes in Hebrew referred to the garments worn by the priest that became blood stained while they were performing their duties of sacrificing. Isn't it interesting that Jesus Christ, our high priest was wrapped in blood stained priest clothes at his birth. (This was prophetic, as Christ is our high priest that shed his blood for our sin and to break every curse. The swaddling clothes were also used for the wicks in the candelabra that were made to keep burning during the Feast of Tabernacles (the menorah was to represent the very presence of God) The candelabras, when burning, lit up the entire region, this was to signify the coming of Messiah, who would be the light of the world. Isn't it interesting, that they did not even recognize him—he was right there in their midst. Do we *really* even recognize the presence of God when he is right here? He said my sheep hear my voice, and they know me. Remember he wants intimacy and a relationship—not religion. He truly is a lamp into our feet and a light into our path. He is our *joy*. The angels sang joy to the world at the birth of Jesus. Interestingly enough, the Feast of Tabernacles is seven days of commanded joy!

The Bible says the joy of the Lord is my strength. Laughter is like a medicine. In his presence is fullness of joy. Thou hast put gladness in my heart, more than in the time that their corn and their wine increased. They that sow in tears shall reap in joy. These things have I spoken unto you, that my joy might remain in you, and that your joy might be full. For then shalt thou have thy delight in the Almighty, and shalt lift up thy face unto God. Yes I will rejoice in the Lord, I will joy in the God of my salvation. My soul shall be satisfied as with marrow and fatness; and my mouth shall praise thee with joyful lips. And thou shalt rejoice in the Lord, and shalt glory in the Holy One of Israel.

Therefore let's purpose right now that we are choosing to be joyful especially for the next seven days. Let's declare a blanket of joy to cover us. Lord *we welcome your joy*!

Right now we are going to partake of the wine. We know this is Jesus blood that was shed for us. But in the Bible, wine is also a symbol of joy and of a marriage covenant; for it was the first miracle that Jesus preformed at the marriage when he turned the water into wine. Lord right now we remember your blood was shed for every area of our healing and we recognize that it is also a symbol of joy and our covenant with you.

Shall we partake? (*Drink the cup*)

As I said earlier, we are commanded to be joyful for seven days. So for the other remaining days I would encourage you to eat together with friends and enjoy the company of others. Attend other sukkot celebrations. Take a walk with a friend, play games, sing, be joyful and laugh! The point is to have lots of fun for seven days.

At this time, let's enjoy some food and fellowship with each other. Can I have my servers to begin to bring the food to the tables, but before we do I will say a prayer of Thanksgiving. (Pray)

You will usually find on Jewish tables a variety of foods, but stuffed foods are extremely common. Stuffed foods are likened to miniature cornucopias, representing a bountiful harvest. God has bountifully blessed us and sealed us with a good year. We are thanking God for our blessings, much like Thanksgiving.

**Make a list of whatever foods you wish to have at your feast**. Ideas, but not contained to these: Tell the guest what you are serving and how they are "stuffed." (Should not include pork or shell fish)

- » First we will be enjoying some ravioli stuffed with cheese and served with a tomato sauce
- » chicken quesadillas (a quesadilla filled with a combination of cheese and chicken)
- » We will be enjoying eggs stuffed with filling
- » There is a trey of bread hollowed out and filled in the center with herbs and balsamic vinegar of Modena and olive oil
- » We have hummus chips with an assortment of artichoke cucina Toscana or pomegranate salsa or garlic dip
- » This trey contains stuffed cream puffs
- » cantaloupe melon hollowed out and stuffed with an assortment of fresh fruit

» and for the sweet tooth: cookies filled with a fig Newton center and covered with powdered sugar

» chocolate hazelnut crème de praline (cookie sticks filled with a chocolate hazelnut filling

» and last we will be having apple blossoms (a light pastry filled with an apple and caramel mixture

Since we are commanded to come together on the first and eighth day, there will be a final shared time together for those that wish to come eight days from now. (One last time) It is a time to recap the feast for the entire year and learn what is significant about the eighth day. I would ask that when you come in eight days that you bring with you a dish of some type of food that pertains to one of the feast. (Recipes can be found on the internet) Be prepared to tell us why you chose this dish or liked its meaning. This will be a time of just having fun and sharing. You may even have a short testimony to share of how God has blessed you by observing the feast.

# An Eighth Day Assembly Preparation List

**Preparation and Food:**

1.   The set up for this assembly is very casual. Have a couple of tables set up for guest to sit their food on as they arrive. Set up tables for guest to sit with table cloths. A simple flower arrangement can be placed on the food tables if desired. Also simple decoration for the guest table if desired; one can be as elaborate as he chooses. The idea of this gathering is to have the **guest bring a dish they have prepared or purchased (pot luck) that represents one of the feasts for the year.** It is fun to have them explain what they have prepared and which feast it represents.

2.   **Have two candles in a holder with a lighter** set on a table, for the lightening of the candles. (Choose a lady of honor to light the candles prior to starting)

3.   Have a place for the speaker to stand

# An Eighth Day Assembly/Shamini Atzerot: The End to a Beginning

## Script for Leader

### Let's pray over the food

Before we eat, I want to ask each of you to give a short description of what kind of food you prepared or brought for tonight and how it relates to one of the feasts' we have celebrated this year.

I will give you time to make your plate and be seated. Since this is an informal gathering tonight, as we eat, if there are any of you that would like to share in any way how these feast have been a blessing to you; feel free at this time. Have you seen results already in ways you feel are related or connected to being obedient in observing the feasts? Hearing about God's blessings might encourage others.

Let's talk about what tonight, the Eighth Day Gathering is all about. I am going to talk as you finish up your meal.

After the High Holy Days of repenting and God atoning for our sin, and an intimate and intense seven days of Sukkot, where we were commanded to be joyful, God's people are now all preparing to return home and get back into the routines of their everyday lives. Our celebrations of the feast are coming to an end.

In Israel, Jewish people are preparing to return to their places of residence. After praising Adoni with the four species, the etrog and the branches, (Remember these were waived in six directions-north, south, east, west, up, and down) and residing in their booths for seven days, they are packing their things up and preparing to leave. It is as if God is saddened that everyone is leaving and the festivities are ending. It will be six months before everyone is gathered together again in the spring for the Feast of Passover. God will miss this close connection with his people. He will miss the sounds of laughter, the reading of the Torah, and joyful music. It's as if God is inviting us to stay one more day.

The purpose of this festival is to review and recap all of the feasts for the year, so that we can make a mental picture of everything we have experienced and learned from the previous days and feasts. It is to glean all of the instruction and knowledge we can from these appointed days of God. It teaches us God's blueprint for blessing his children throughout the year. It also teaches us about true repentance and forgiveness, so that He can set us free from bondage and wipe our slate clean. He then can in turn give us abundant joy and prosperity in every area of our lives for the coming year.

You see, the Eighth Day Gathering is about an intimate and close relationship with our creator God.

These feasts have had a lot of important meaning and symbolism. We have eaten different foods and have done things that help us remember the specific feasts, and blessings that are connected to them; but the most important thing is our relationship with Him. While all of these things we have done have been fun and helpful, what is most pressing to God is the intimate time we have spent with Him and in His presence. God wants to draw us closer and show us his heart. He wants us to see his infinite love for us. This gathering is likened to a bride and groom's wedding after the guest have gone and they share intimate time together. After Sukkot is over, and the "should we say guest" or fall harvest has been gathered, the bride or body of Christ and the groom—Yeshua Messiah—will have intimate time for themselves. This day brings an even deeper expression of love.

Our Messiah is saying: I am my beloved, and he is mine.

> Note: Let's start by honoring God with the lightening of the candles, ushering in his presence. (Woman of honor lights the candle.)[17]

This time, on God's calendar, is the beginning of the rainy season. The people of Israel say a prayer for God to send an abundance of rain so the earth will be wet and able to produce.

In reference to the feast, there is a former and a latter rain. The Holy Spirit is a type of spiritual rain. God always does things in the spiritual and in the natural. God we petition you right now to bring a down pour of your Holy Spirit rain into our lives and saturate the soil of our hearts and every part of the dry, parched areas of our lives. We want you to replenish, refresh and restore every one of us to overflowing.

Joel 2: 28-29 says this:

*Reader #1*** And it shall come to pass afterward, that I will pour out my spirit upon all flesh; and your sons and your daughters shall prophesy, your old men shall dream dreams, your young men shall see visions; And also upon the servants and upon the handmaids in those days will I pour out my spirit. (KJV)

God wants to pour out his Holy Spirit on everyone. He doesn't want to be separated from you any longer! He desires to dwell inside of you and be a part of you forever.

Rain is water, and water itself is a necessity of life. We wouldn't survive very long without water. Our bodies are made up of about 80% water. Water is an essential need to stay alive.

We need the Holy Spirit to sustain life as well. Psalms 42: 1-3 says:

---

17  Have the woman come forward and light the candles

*Reader#2*** As the deer pants for the streams of water, so my soul pants for you, O God. My soul thirsts for God, for the living God. When can I go and meet with God? My tears have been my food day and night, while men say to me, all day long, "Where is your God?"(NIV)

*Reader#3***—Isaiah 55:1 says: "COME, ALL you who are thirsty, come to the waters; and you who have no money, come, buy and eat! Come; buy wine and milk without money and without cost. (NIV)

Let's see how God compares his word to how the rain saturates and waters the earth

*Reader #4—Isaiah 55: 10-13 says: As the rain and the snow come down from heaven, and do not return to it without watering the earth and making it bud and flourish, so that it yields seed for the sower and bread for the eater, so is my word that goes out from my mouth: It will not return to me empty, but will accomplish what I desire and achieve the purpose for which I sent it. You will go out in joy and be lead forth in peace; the mountains and hills will clap their hands. Instead of the thorn bush will grow the pine tree, and instead of the briers the myrtle will grow. This will be for the Lord's renown, for an everlasting sign, which will not be destroyed. (NIV)

*Reader #5—John 4:10 says: Jesus answered her, "If you knew the gift of God and who it is that asks you for a drink, you would have asked him and he would have given you water." (NIV)

*Reader #6—John 4:14 says: but whoever drinks the water I give him will never thirst. Indeed, the water I give him will became in him a spring of water welling up to eternal life." (NIV)

*Reader#7—Isaiah 44:3—For I will pour water on the thirsty land, and streams on the dry ground. I will pour out my Spirit on your offspring, and my blessing on your descendants. They will spring up like grass in a meadow, like poplar trees by flowing streams. (NIV)

*Reader#8—John 7: 37-39 says: In the last day, that great day of the feast, Jesus stood and cried, saying, If any man thirst, let him come unto me, and drink. He that believeth on me, as the scripture hath said, out of his belly shall flow rivers of living water. (But this spake he of the Spirit, which they that believe on him should receive: for the Holy Ghost was not yet given; because that Jesus was not yet glorified.) (KJV)

Let's take a moment right now to *pray*.......that the Holy Spirit will rain down on our land and our nation that is dry and barren; and let's pray God will rain down his Holy Spirit on us, his people that are so thirsty and in such need of an outpouring of his presence.

We celebrated Sukkot for seven days. This completes the harvest festival. But tonight represents the final day of harvesting and ingathering. The eighth day gathering is the completion of God's plan for mankind. It is the completion of salvation, or in Hebrew, so-zoed: meaning not just saved from sin, but a continual process of being restored, redeemed, healed, and set free, from curses and bondage. It was a complete work.

So why would God want us to meet again on the eighth day?

What is significant or special about the number eight?

The number eight signifies that which is above the natural cycle. (Example: Like the world to come-the periods after the one thousand year reign. Remember the feast of tabernacles represented the one thousand year reign of Jesus Christ, which was a feast that lasted for seven days. Now we come to the eighth day which represents the period after the one thousand year reign. Eight also means the beginning of another world. It is the beginning of another world spent in eternity with our savior. A perfect world as He intended it to be from the beginning. He longs to spend time with us as He did with Adam and Eve in the Garden.

The number eight symbolizes *release*. Rabbinical teaching says that when the tabernacle was completed, the Lord's presence was revealed on the eighth day…Wander why He chose to wait until the eighth day to reveal himself? The number eight is symbolic of completion. The work was completed prior;

but God was saying, now, on the eighth day, the day of completion, it is not only complete but indeed, totally complete by the presence of God being revealed. Lord, reveal and release your presence right now, on our Eighth Day Gathering. We want you to pour yourself out on us as we honor you and spend intimate time with you.

In Jewish study, there is a deeper way of studying the Bible. Each letter is assigned a number; such as the letter "A" might be "one", "B" is two and so forth. They add these numbers together for a deeper meaning. That is why it is very important not to add or take away from the Bible. God is very precise and exact in everything He does. God's ways are so perfect. Yeshua's Hebrew name by Gematria= 386, however in Greek—Jesus name by Gematria= 888. Remember nothing is a coincidence with God. His word is perfect in every way.

David was the eighth son of Jesse thus beginning a new dynasty in Israel when he became King. And we know Jesus Christ came from the lineage of David.

The number eight represents resurrection and a new beginning. In Matthew 28:1, on the eighth day Mary Magdalene and the other Mary came to see the tomb. In John 20:26, after eight days the disciples and Thomas were in the room and they saw Jesus when He came through the door and stood in their midst, and said, "Peace to You!" This was when he allowed Thomas to touch his scars, because he was in doubt. The number eight marks a new beginning. According to God's calendar, we are entering a New Year. We too can begin with a clean slate and a new start in life. God wants you free indeed! But the last significant thing I want to mention that is connected with the number eight is that if you remember, we said Jesus was born on the Feast of Tabernacles.

It is Jewish custom to be circumcised on the eighth day following the birth of a child. Circumcision is a symbol of the covenant made between God and the Jewish people. They wait eight days to circumcise a male child as the child will have been through a complete week which includes a Sabbath; he may then enter into the covenant of the Jewish people. Remember Sukkot is when Jesus Christ was born. There is seven days of commanded joy, which brings us to the eighth day. Jesus Christ was probably circumcised on the eighth day. It is thought in Jewish traditions that Adam was born without a foreskin. When Adam sinned, it created a barrier between him and God, therefore from then on a foreskin developed. When the foreskin was removed at birth, it represented a physical attempt by man to return or come back to God. Brisnila—means circumcism bris—means covenant. Isn't it remarkable to think that Jesus Christ himself was circumcised on this day, establishing his everlasting covenant with us.

Let's recap the feast this year. The first feast we celebrated was Passover. Passover means, protection. The three elements were, bitter herbs and unleavened bread, and a spotless lamb. We remember His bitter sacrifice; we are to rid ourselves of leaven, which is a type of pride. Pride can cause us to be puffed up and arrogant, which is not of God. We are to remember Jesus Christ gave himself as the ultimate, spotless Lamb. Just as he brought his people out of bondage in Egypt, He has freed us from the bondage of sin by Jesus Christ making a blood covenant with mankind when he gave Himself on the cross. This is also one of the Biblical times we are told to bring an offering before the Lord.

The next was the Feast of Pentecost. This was the ingathering of the First Harvest. This was also the time when the Ten Commandments were given on Mt. Sinai in the Old Testament fifty days after leaving Egypt; then the infilling of the Holy Spirit was given in the New Testament exactly fifty days after the death of Jesus Christ on the cross. This is also a time to give our second offering to God.

Next, is the Fall Festivals, which pictures the Wedding Ceremony of the Church as compared to a Jewish wedding. The first fall Feast of Rosh Hashanah, or Trumpets is the call to repentance; it causes us to search our hearts of any wrong doing and to ask forgiveness. The blowing shofar of warning, tells us to get ready for the coming of The Lord. It is also the birthday of Adam and Eve.

Then the holiest day of the year, the Day of Atonement, is when we are "at one" with God. The Day of Atonement is a picture of Jesus Christ shedding His blood as atonement for our sin. We are to fast on this day. It causes us to seek forgiveness so our Heavenly Father can forgive us and seal us for another good year if he tarries. He indeed became our supreme sacrifice; therefore we no longer sacrifice lambs and bulls. We are to give ourselves as a living sacrifice, holy and acceptable unto Him.

The seven day Feast of Sukkot or Ingathering, which is also known as The Feast of Tabernacles, is the final feast that pictures the millennial reign of Messiah for one thousand years. It is the actual time of Jesus' birth, although some celebrate this in December. Sukkot in Hebrew means stable. We are told to construct a temporary booth in this feast to remember how God supplied every need for the Israelites in the dessert and how He wants to tabernacle, or live in us forever. We are to be joyful and have fun for seven days, while waving the four species and etrog in six directions, symbolizing God is everywhere. This is the time for our third and final offering.

The Eighth Day Gathering pictures the completion of salvation. Being so-zoed completes His work of healing us, prospering us and freeing us. It also pictures the Great White Throne Judgment that occurs at the end of the millennium. It is as if God is saying, "let's spend one more day together-He is looking for intimacy in a relationship, not a religion. It is when He would have been circumcised according to Jewish custom—symbolizing a covenant and completion of a human being. The eighth day represents a state of perfection—This symbolizes the new Heaven and New Earth coming down.

As I have said in the past festivals, I believe God is now opening the eyes of the Gentile people, to a revelation in scripture that has been there all along but hidden all these years, and saved for the very end of times to fulfill scripture and prophecy. I believe remembering and celebrating the Feast of God is going to bring so much blessing that others will see and want to know how we are so blessed in a world and economy that is collapsing. We can tell them that we have discovered our need to return to our Jewish heritage and to partake in God's Feast and Holy Days. He commanded us to teach these Feasts to our children from generation to generation. As a result of our obedience, he will cause great blessing and abundance in our lives. In turn, as the world catches on, it will provoke the Jews to also see the blessing God has put on the Gentile people and will provoke them to jealousy. Thus, in the end bringing Gentile and Jew together into one new man, which is God's ultimate goal. Praise God we are actually living out and taking part in Bible Prophecy. What an exciting time to live in!

# PART THREE:
# RESOURCES & MATERIALS

# Re-printable Sheets: The Feast of Passover, Unleavened Bread and Firstfruits

Reader # 1 Do not forget that you are Gentiles. In fact, you used to be called "uncircumcised" by those who take pride in being circumcised. At that time you did not know about Christ. You were foreigners to the people of Israel, and you had no part in the promise that God had made to them. You were living in this world without hope and without God, and you were far from God. But Christ offered his life's blood as a sacrifice and brought you near God. Christ has made peace between Jews and Gentiles, and he has united us by breaking down the wall of hatred that separated us. Christ gave his own body to destroy the Law of Moses with all its rules and commands. (the law of commandments contained in ordinances. New King James Version) He even brought Jews and Gentiles together as though we were only one person, when he united us in peace. On the cross Christ did away with our hatred for each other. He also made peace between us and God by uniting Jews and Gentiles in one body. Christ came and preached peace to you Gentiles, who were far from God, and peace to Jews, who were near God. And because of Christ, all of us can come to the Father by the same Spirit. You Gentiles are no longer strangers and foreigners. You are citizens with everyone else who belongs to the family of God. You are like a building with the apostles and prophets as the foundation and with Christ as the most important stone. Christ is the one who holds the building together and makes it grow into a holy temple for the Lord. And you are part of that building Christ has built as a place for God's own Spirit to live.

READER #2 Romans 11:17-18 says it this way in the Contemporary English version: You Gentiles are like branches of a wild olive tree that were made to be part of a cultivated olive tree. You have taken the place of some branches that were cut away from it. And because of this, you enjoy the blessings that come from being part of that cultivated tree. But don't think you are better than the branches that were cut away. Just remember that you are not supporting the roots of that tree. Its roots are supporting you.

# Blessings for Passover

*Lighting of Candles*

Blessed art thou O Lord, King of the Universe, who has sanctified us in His commandments, and commanded us to kindle the Passover lights.

*Cup of Sanctification*

Blessed art thou our God, King of the Universe, who has preserved us alive, sustained us, and brought us to enjoy this season.

*Second Cup*

Blessed art thou O Lord our God, King of the Universe, creator of the fruit of the vine.

*Third Cup of Redemption/Communion Cup*

Blessed art thou O Lord our God, King of the Universe, creator of the fruit of the vine.

*Fourth Cup/Cup of Praise*

Blessed art thou O Lord our God, King of the Universe, creator of the fruit of the vine

# THE TEN PLAGUES

1. PLAGUE OF BLOOD ON THE WATERS
2. PLAGUE OF FROGS THAT COVERED THE LANDS
3. PLAGUE OF GNATS THAT CAME UPON THE MEN AND THE ANIMALS
4. PLAGUE OF FLIES THAT CAME UPON THE PEOPLE AND THEIR HOMES
5. PLAGUE ON THE LIVESTOCK OF THE EGYPTIANS [KILLING THEIR LIVESTOCK]
6. PLAGUE OF FESTERING BOILS ON THE MEN AND ANIMALS
7. PLAGUE OF HAIL, DESTROYING THEIR LAND AND CROPS
8. PLAGUE OF LOCUST ON THE GROUNDS, ERADICATING WHAT REMAINED
9. PLAGUE OF DARKNESS COVERING EGYPT FOR A TOTAL OF THREE DAYS
10. PLAGUE OF THE FIRSTBORN [KILLING OF EVERY FIRSTBORN SON IN EGYPT]

# THE TEN PLAGUES

1. PLAGUE OF BLOOD ON THE WATERS
2. PLAGUE OF FROGS THAT COVERED THE LANDS
3. PLAGUE OF GNATS THAT CAME UPON THE MEN AND THE ANIMALS
4. PLAGUE OF FLIES THAT CAME UPON THE PEOPLE AND THEIR HOMES
5. PLAGUE ON THE LIVESTOCK OF THE EGYPTIANS [KILLING THEIR LIVESTOCK]
6. PLAGUE OF FESTERING BOILS ON THE MEN AND ANIMALS
7. PLAGUE OF HAIL, DESTROYING THEIR LAND AND CROPS
8. PLAGUE OF LOCUST ON THE GROUNDS, ERADICATING WHAT REMAINED
9. PLAGUE OF DARKNESS COVERING EGYPT FOR A TOTAL OF THREE DAYS
10. PLAGUE OF THE FIRSTBORN [KILLING OF EVERY FIRSTBORN SON IN EGYPT]

# THE TEN PLAGUES

1. PLAGUE OF BLOOD ON THE WATERS
2. PLAGUE OF FROGS THAT COVERED THE LANDS
3. PLAGUE OF GNATS THAT CAME UPON THE MEN AND THE ANIMALS
4. PLAGUE OF FLIES THAT CAME UPON THE PEOPLE AND THEIR HOMES
5. PLAGUE ON THE LIVESTOCK OF THE EGYPTIANS [KILLING THEIR LIVESTOCK]
6. PLAGUE OF FESTERING BOILS ON THE MEN AND ANIMALS
7. PLAGUE OF HAIL, DESTROYING THEIR LAND AND CROPS
8. PLAGUE OF LOCUST ON THE GROUNDS, ERADICATING WHAT REMAINED
9. PLAGUE OF DARKNESS COVERING EGYPT FOR A TOTAL OF THREE DAYS
10. PLAGUE OF THE FIRSTBORN [KILLING OF EVERY FIRSTBORN SON IN EGYPT]

# Re-printable Sheets: The Feast of Pentecost

(Reader #1) **Then you shall keep the Feast of Weeks to the LORD your God with the tribute of a freewill offering from your hand, which you shall give as the LORD your God blesses you. And you shall rejoice before the LORD your God, you, and your son and your daughter, your male servant and your female servant, the Levite who is within your towns, the sojourner, the fatherless and the widow who are among you, at the place that the LORD your God will choose, to make his name dwell there. Deuteronomy 16: 10-11 (ESV)

***Reader #2 Acts 2:1-21 (TMB) And when the day of Pentecost was fully come, they were all with one accord in one place. And suddenly there came a sound from heaven as of a rushing mighty wind, and it filled all the house where they were sitting. And there appeared unto them cloven tongues like as of fire, and it sat upon each of them. And they were all filled with the Holy Ghost, and began to speak with other tongues, as the Spirit gave them utterance. And there were dwelling at Jerusalem Jews, devout men, out of every nation under heaven. Now when this was noised abroad, the multitude came together, and was confounded, because that every man heard them speak in his own language. And they were all amazed and marveled, saying one to another, Behold, are not all these which speak Galileans? And how hear we every man in our own tongue, wherein we were born?

(Then skip down to verse 12) And they were all amazed, and were in doubt, saying one to another. What meanest this? Others mocking said, these men are full of new wine. But Peter, standing up with the eleven, lifted up his voice, and said unto them. Ye men of Judaea, and all ye that dwell at Jerusalem, be this known unto you, and hearken to my words. For these are not drunken, as ye suppose, seeing it is but the third hour of the day. But this is that which was spoken by the prophet Joel; And it shall come to pass in the last days, saith God, I will pour out of my Spirit upon all flesh: and your sons and your daughters shall prophesy, and your young men shall see visions, and your old men shall dream dreams: And on my servants and on my handmaidens I will pour out in those days of my Spirit: and they shall prophesy: And I will show wonders in heaven above, and signs in the earth beneath: blood, and fire, and vapor of smoke: The sun shall be turned into darkness, and the moon into blood, before that great and notable day of the Lord come: And it shall come to pass that whosoever shall call on the name of the Lord shall be saved.

# PENTECOST COMPARISON SHEET

| OLD TESTAMENT | NEW TESTAMENT |
|---|---|
| Israel came out of bondage and exactly fifty days later were given the *Ten Commandments*. | Jesus died, and arose, and exactly fifty days later, God sent the Holy Spirit. |
| Commandments of God were written on Tablets of Stone.<br><br>[Exodus 24:12] | Commandments of God were written on the heart.<br><br>[Jeremiah 31:33, Psalm 40:8, Psalm 37:31, Isaiah 51:7, Ezekiel 11:19-20, Ezekiel 36:22-27, 2 Corinthians 3:3, Hebrews 8:10] |
| Commandments written by the Finger of God.<br><br>[Exodus 31:18] | Commandments written by the Spirit of God<br><br>[2 Corinthians 3:3, Hebrew 8:10] |
| Three thousand were slain.<br><br>[Exodus 32:1-8, Exodus 32:26-28] | Three Thousand live<br><br>[Acts 2:38-41] |
| The Letter of The Torah | The Spirit of The Torah<br><br>[Romans 2:29, Romans 7:6, 2 Corinthians 3:6] |
| Mount Sinai<br><br>[Exodus 19:11, Hebrews 12:22, 1 Peter 2:6] | Mount Zion<br><br>[Romans 11:26] |
| When Israel came to Mount Sinai, it was the first time in Torah, Israel was referred to in the singular-as in one person.<br><br>[Exodus 19:1-29]<br><br>*The last sentence in the verse, the verb in Hebrew is in the singular* | All with one accord, one place<br><br>[Acts 2:1] |
| A Harvest Feast celebrating the In-Gathering of the First Harvest. | As a result of the in-filling of the Holy Spirit, three-thousand people were born again on the same day. This was the First Harvest unto The Lord.<br><br>[Acts 2:41] |

# THE TEN COMMANDMENTS

1. THOU SHALT HAVE NO OTHER GOD'S BEFORE ME
2. THOU SHALT NOT MAKE UNTO THEE ANY GRAVEN IMAGE
3. THOU SHALT NOT TAKE THE NAME OF THE LORD THY GOD IN VAIN
4. REMEMBER THE SABBATH DAY, TO KEEP IT HOLY
5. HONOUR THY FATHER AND MOTHER
6. THOU SHALT NOT KILL
7. THOU SHALT NOT COMMIT ADULTERY
8. THOU SHALT NOT STEAL
9. THOU SHALT NOT BEAR FALSE WITNESS AGAINST THY NEIGHBOUR
10. THOU SHALT NOT COVET

# THE TEN COMMANDMENTS

1. THOU SHALT HAVE NO OTHER GOD'S BEFORE ME
2. THOU SHALT NOT MAKE UNTO THEE ANY GRAVEN IMAGE
3. THOU SHALT NOT TAKE THE NAME OF THE LORD THY GOD IN VAIN
4. REMEMBER THE SABBATH DAY, TO KEEP IT HOLY
5. HONOUR THY FATHER AND MOTHER
6. THOU SHALT NOT KILL
7. THOU SHALT NOT COMMIT ADULTERY
8. THOU SHALT NOT STEAL
9. THOU SHALT NOT BEAR FALSE WITNESS AGAINST THY NEIGHBOUR
10. THOU SHALT NOT COVET

# THE TEN COMMANDMENTS

1. THOU SHALT HAVE NO OTHER GOD'S BEFORE ME
2. THOU SHALT NOT MAKE UNTO THEE ANY GRAVEN IMAGE
3. THOU SHALT NOT TAKE THE NAME OF THE LORD THY GOD IN VAIN
4. REMEMBER THE SABBATH DAY, TO KEEP IT HOLY
5. HONOUR THY FATHER AND MOTHER
6. THOU SHALT NOT KILL
7. THOU SHALT NOT COMMIT ADULTERY
8. THOU SHALT NOT STEAL
9. THOU SHALT NOT BEAR FALSE WITNESS AGAINST THY NEIGHBOUR
10. THOU SHALT NOT COVET

# Sanctuary Readings

**Pastor**: Now if there is anyone who desires to give an offering come forward at this time and place it in the basket that has been prepared

\*\*\* **(Pastor)** let's make our confession

\*\*\***Everyone Repeat**: I confess this day unto the Lord thy God that I have come unto the country which the Lord swore unto our fathers (Abraham, Isaac, and Jacob) to give us.

\*\*\***Pastor:** I will set this offering before the Lord. Let's speak and say before the Lord our God

\*\*\***Everyone repeats:** We praise the Lord for all the things that Jesus Christ has brought us through. You are taking us out of slavery and bringing us into the land that God promised in the Abrahamic Covenant

\*\*\***Pastor:** Right now as we confess to the Lord what he has done for us and delivered us from, we are recognizing and acknowledging with our profession combined with our first fruit offering that Jehovah God is the source of everything we have. God not only gives; He also sustains and keeps us. And as we do this and bring our offering, we are actually setting this before the Lord. "WE SET IT." Take a few minutes to confess to God what he has done for you in your life.

(Take a few minutes)

***Pastor**: Look down on us and bless your people, and the land which thou hast given, as thou swarest unto our fathers, a land that floweth with milk and honey. This day the Lord thy God commanded thee to do these statutes and judgments: thou shalt therefore keep and do them with all thine heart, and with all thy soul. You have asked the Lord this day to be thy God, and to walk in his ways, and to keep his statutes, and his commandments, and his judgments, and to hearken unto his voice: And the LORD hath avouched thee this day to be his peculiar people, as he hath promised thee, and thou shouldest keep all his commandments: And to make thee high above all nations which he hath made, in praise, and in name, and in honor; and that thou mayest be an holy people unto the LORD thy God, as he hath spoken.

Now as we have been obedient and acted upon His word, our God is obligated based on the Abrahamic Covenant, to see us through.

***Pastor:** Now if I could have EVERYONE come forward and stand together.

I would like to anoint everyone's hands for prosperity. (Anoint everyone's hands at one time—then pray)

Now, I want to lay hands on everyone's forehead for wisdom and the gifts of the Holy Spirit. (Anoint everyone's forehead at one time, and say a corporate prayer that all curses are broken off our lives and that all debt is cancelled.)

# Re-printable Sheets: The Feast of Trumpets

*Blessed are you Lord our God, King of the universe, who creates the fruit of the vine*

(Reader 1) "I know your works, that you are neither cold nor hot. I could wish you were cold or hot. So then, because you are lukewarm, and neither cold nor hot, will I vomit you out of My mouth. (NKJV)

(Reader 2) …as a man chasteneth his son, so the LORD thy God chasteneth thee. (KJV)

(Reader 3)** And at midnight a cry was heard: "Behold the bridegroom is coming; go out to meet him!" Then all those virgins arose and trimmed their lamps. And the foolish said to the wise, "Give us some of your oil, for our lamps are going out." But the wise answered, saying, "No, lest there should not be enough for us and you; but go rather to those that sell, and buy for yourselves." And while they went to buy, the bridegroom came, and those who were ready went in with him to the wedding; and the door was shut. Afterward the other virgins came also saying, "Lord, Lord, open to us!" But he answered and said, "Assuredly, I say to you, I do not know you." Matthew 25:6-12 (NKJV)

(Reader 4)***Let us be glad and rejoice, and give honor to him for the marriage of the Lamb is come, and his wife hath made herself ready. And to her was granted that she should be arrayed in fine linen, clean and white for the fine linen is the righteousness of saints. And he saith unto me, Write blessed are they which are called unto the marriage supper of the Lamb. And he saith unto me. These are the true sayings of God. (NKJV)

(Reader 5)** Turn from evil and do good; seek peace and pursue it.(NIV)

(Reader 6) "Wake up! Hear the sound of the trumpet. Let it awaken you out of your sleep, because if you are asleep, you are not redeeming the time. The King is coming; the Bridegroom is coming; wake up, because when He comes and finds you asleep, and you say, "Lord, don't forget me," it will be too late."

(Reader 7) Three times in a year shall all thy males shall appear before the Lord thy God in the place which he shall choose; in the feast of unleavened bread, and in the feast of weeks, and in the feast of tabernacles: and they shall not appear before the Lord empty: Every man shall give as he is able, according to the blessing of the Lord thy God which he hath given thee. (KJV)

# Re-printable Sheet: The Day of Atonement

**Reader #1 ****Moreover when ye fast, be not, as the hypocrites, of a sad countenance: for they disfigure their faces, that they may appear unto men to fast. Verily I say unto you, They have their reward. But thou, when thou fastest, anoint thine head, and wash thy face; That thou appear not unto men to fast, but unto thy Father which is in secret: and thy Father, which seeth in secret, shall reward thee openly. (JKV)***

Reader #2 *** "Even now," declares the Lord, "return to me with all your heart, with fasting and weeping and morning." Rend your heart and not your garments, Return to the Lord your God, for he is gracious and compassionate, slow to anger and abounding in love,and he relents from sending calamity. Who knows? He may turn and have pity and leave behind a blessing—grain offerings and drink offerings for the Lord your God.

Reader #3 ***Blow the trumpet in Zion. Declare a holy fast, call a sacred assembly. Gather the people, consecrate the assembly; bring together the elders, gather the children, those nursing at the breast. Let the bridegroom leave his room and the bride her chamber. Let the priests, the minister before the LORD, weep between the temple porch and the alter. Let them say, "Spare your people, O LORD, Do not make your inheritance an object of scorn, a byword among the nations. Why should they say among the peoples, Where is their God?" Then the LORD will be jealous for his land and take pity on his people. The LORD will reply to them: I am sending you grain, new wine and oil, enough to satisfy you fully: never again will I make you an object of scorn to the nations. I will drive the northern army far from you, pushing it into a parched and barren land, with its front columns going into the eastern sea and those in the rear into the western sea. And its stench will go up; its smell will rise." Surely he has done great things. Be not afraid, O land; be glad and rejoice. Surely the LORD has done great things. Be not afraid, O wild animals, for the open pastures are becoming green. The trees are bearing their fruit; the fig tree and the vine yield their riches. Be glad, O people of Zion, rejoice in the LORD your God, for he has given you the autumn rains in righteousness. He sends you abundant showers, both autumn and spring rains, as before. The threshing floors will be filled with grain; the vats will overflow with new wine and oil. "I will repay you for the years the locust swarm—my great army that I sent among you. You will have plenty to eat, until you are full, and you will praise the name of the LORD your God, who has worked wonders for you; never again will my people be ashamed. Then you will know that I am in Israel, that I am the LORD your God, and that there is no other; never again will my people be shamed. Joel 2: 15-27 (NIV)

Reader #4 **"And afterward, I will pour out my Spirit on all people. Your sons and daughters will prophesy, your old men will dream dreams, your young men will see visions. Even on my servants, both men and women, I will pour out my Spirit in those days. I will show wonders in the heavens and on the earth, blood and fire and billows of smoke. The sun will be turned to darkness and the moon to blood before the coming of the great and dreadful day of the LORD. Joel 2: 28-31 (NIV)

# ***Blessing***
## ** Hear O Israel, the Lord is Our God, the Lord is One**
## Areas of prayer:

**1- Renounce and reverse any generational curses that might have been brought on your life by you or an ancestor or parent. 2- REPENT FOR THE SIN. 3- Forgive and release them for passing on the sin. 4- Place the blood of the cross over it and command the sin of _____ and all accompanying curses to be stopped. 5- Allow freedom and healing to be released. 6. Reverse the curse by speaking blessing into your life (the opposite of the generational curse)

**1- Sever ungodly soul ties or ungodly relationships from your past or that are now in the present—just the ungodly part—not the relationship itself. (This could involve past or present sexual partners or friends and family members that have caused hurt creating an ungodly tie) 2-Confess and release the ungodly soul tie with _____. #3- Forgive ___, and forgive yourself. #4- I sever the ungodly soul tie and ask God to restore the broken portions and remove anything that has come into me through the soul tie. Lord bring back the Godly part that was stolen.

**1-Replace beliefs that is negative. #2-Repent of the sin (or ancestors sin) of negative beliefs or expectations. #3-I forgive ___ for causing me to form a wrong view or negative belief about this person or institution. #4- I believe and confess that _____ is the truth.

**1- I renounce inner vows that I have made. #2- I confess the sin of vowing_____. #3-I forgive _____for contributing to my forming this vow and I forgive myself. #4-I now purpose to believe that_____.

**1-Healing of deep wounds that have caused traumatic pictures. #2-Confess and repent of bitterness and anger toward God for allowing this to happen. #3-I receive forgiveness and I forgive myself for any involvement. #4-Lord help me to see the scene knowing that you were there (people are given a free will, but it is NOT God's will for hurt to occur) #5- Lord I curse the "cellular memory" to be gone from this traumatic event. #6- I speak healing and complete wholeness over the traumatic event of ___.

**1-Break word curses off. Example: He makes me sick or I will NEVER be able to do___ #2- Confess and repent for taking on the word curse that I ___ and for my anger. #3- I forgive and release ___(or myself) for speaking this over me. #4- I accept your divine deliverance and break this curse off of me by the blood of Jesus Christ. I receive the blessing of ___(opposite of) which replaces the curse.

**1-Casting out of an unclean spirit. #2- pray through previous prayers and repent. #3- In the name and by the blood of Jesus Christ, I renounce and break all strongholds of _____off of my life. #4-I am bought by the blood of Jesus Christ and take authority over the unclean spirit of ___. I bind you and command you to leave me in the name of the Lord Jesus Christ. I do not want you. I am blood bought property. Tell God that you no longer want these things to keep you in bondage, and to take them away from you and set you free. Remember when we apply the blood; the devil cannot penetrate the blood covering. He no longer has a hold on you. We are redeemed by the blood. You may need a spirit filled person praying with you.

# Re-printable Sheet: The Feast of Tabernacles/Rosh Hashanah

**Reader#1 And it shall come to pass, that every one that is left of all the nations which came against Jerusalem shall even go up from year to year to worship the King, the Lord of hosts, and to keep the feast of tabernacles. (KJV)**

** Reader #2***"Thou shalt observe the feast of tabernacles seven days, after that thou hast gathered in thy corn and thy wine: And thou shalt rejoice in thy feast, thou, and thy son, and thy daughter….Seven days shalt thou keep a solemn feast unto the Lord thy God in the place which the Lord shall choose: because the Lord thy God shall bless thee in all thine increase, and in all the works of thine hands, therefore thou shalt surely rejoice… and they shall not appear before the Lord empty: Every man shall give as he is able, according to the blessing of the Lord thy God which he hath given thee. (KJV) Deut. 16: 13-17.

**Reader #3*** …Test me in this," says the Lord Almighty," and see if I will not throw open the floodgates of heaven and pour out so much blessing that you will not have room enough for it." Malachi 3: 10 (NIV)

# Re-printable Sheet: The Eighth Day Feast

*Reader #1*** And it shall come to pass afterward, that I will pour out my spirit upon all flesh; and your sons and your daughters shall prophesy, your old men shall dream dreams, your young men shall see visions; And also upon the servants and upon the handmaids in those days will I pour out my spirit. (KJV)

*Reader#2*** As the deer pants for the streams of water, so my soul pants for you, O God. My soul thirsts for God, for the living God. When can I go and meet with God? My tears have been my food day and night, while men say to me, all day long, "Where is your God?"(NIV)

*Reader#3***—Isaiah 55:1 says: "COME, ALL you who are thirsty, come to the waters; and you who have no money, come, buy and eat! Come; buy wine and milk without money and without cost. (NIV)

*Reader #4—Isaiah 55: 10-13 says: As the rain and the snow come down from heaven, and do not return to it without watering the earth and making it bud and flourish, so that it yields seed for the sower and bread for the eater, so is my word that goes out from my mouth: It will not return to me empty, but will accomplish what I desire and achieve the purpose for which I sent it. You will go out in joy and be lead forth in peace; the mountains and hills will clap their hands. Instead of the thorn bush will grow the pine tree, and instead of the briers the myrtle will grow. This will be for the Lord's renown, for an everlasting sign, which will not be destroyed. (NIV)

*Reader #5—John 4:10 says: Jesus answered her, "If you knew the gift of God and who it is that asks you for a drink, you would have asked him and he would have given you water." (NIV)

*Reader #6—John 4:14 says: but whoever drinks the water I give him will never thirst. Indeed, the water I give him will became in him a spring of water welling up to eternal life." (NIV)

*Reader#7—Isaiah 44:3—For I will pour water on the thirsty land, and streams on the dry ground. I will pour out my Spirit on your offspring, and my blessing on your descendants. They will spring up like grass in a meadow, like poplar trees by flowing streams. (NIV)

*Reader#8—John 7: 37-39 says: In the last day, that great day of the feast, Jesus stood and cried, saying, If any man thirst, let him come unto me, and drink. He that believeth on me, as the scripture hath said, out of his belly shall flow rivers of living water. (But this spake he of the Spirit, which they that believe on him should receive: for the Holy Ghost was not yet given; because that Jesus was not yet glorified.) (KJV)

# CALENDAR OF GOD'S FEASTS

## PESACH
### PASSOVER | UNLEAVENED BREAD | FIRSTFRUITS OFFERING

| REMEMBERING THE EXODUS | | |
|---|---|---|
| APRIL | 15-22 | 2014 |
| APRIL | 04-11 | 2015 |
| APRIL | 23-30 | 2016 |
| APRIL | 11-18 | 2017 |

## SHAVOUT
### THE FEAST OF PENTECOST

| THE TEN COMMANDMENTS WERE GIVEN | THE HOLY SPIRIT CAME | |
|---|---|---|
| JUNE | 04-05 | 2014 |
| MAY | 24-25 | 2015 |
| JUNE | 12-13 | 2016 |
| MAY-JUNE | 31-01 | 2017 |

## ROSH HASHANAH
### THE FEAST OF TRUMPETS

| THE JEWISH NEW YEAR | THE COMING OF THE MESSIAH | |
|---|---|---|
| SEPTEMBER | 25-26 | 2014 |
| SEPTEMBER | 14-15 | 2015 |
| OCTOBER | 03-04 | 2016 |
| SEPTEMBER | 21-22 | 2017 |

## YOM KIPPUR
### DAY OF ATTONEMENT

| BLOOD COVENANT | | |
|---|---|---|
| OCTOBER | 04 | 2014 |
| SEPTEMBER | 23 | 2015 |
| OCTOBER | 12 | 2016 |
| SEPTEMBER | 30 | 2017 |

## SUKKOT
### THE FEAST OF TABERNACLES

| THE HARVEST FESTIVAL | | |
|---|---|---|
| OCTOBER | 09-15 | 2014 |
| SEPTEMBER-OCTOBER | 28-04 | 2015 |
| OCTOBER | 17-23 | 2016 |
| OCTOBER | 05-11 | 2017 |

## SHAMINI ATZERET
### AN EIGHTH DAY ASSEMBLY

| COMPLETION | | |
|---|---|---|
| OCTOBER | 16 | 2014 |
| OCTOBER | 5 | 2015 |
| OCTOBER | 24 | 2016 |
| OCTOBER | 12 | 2017 |